THE WISDOM
OF
HARVEY PENICK

—————

*Lessons and Thoughts
from the Collected Writings of
Golf's Best-Loved Teacher*

HARVEY PENICK *with* BUD SHRAKE

—————

SIMON & SCHUSTER
New York London Toronto Sydney

SIMON & SCHUSTER
1230 Avenue of the Americas
New York, NY 10020

This Simon & Schuster hardcover edition March 2010

SIMON & SCHUSTER and colophon are registered
trademarks of Simon & Schuster Inc.

For information about special discounts for bulk purchases,
please contact Simon & Schuster Special Sales at
1-866-506-1949 or business@simonandschuster.com.

The Simon & Schuster Speakers Bureau can bring authors
to your live event. For more information or to book an event,
contact the Simon & Schuster Speakers Bureau at
1-866-248-3049 or visit our website at www.simonspeakers.com.

Designed by Helene Berinsky

Manufactured in the United States of America

10   9   8   7   6   5   4   3   2   1

Library of Congress Cataloging-in-Publication Data
Penick, Harvey.
The wisdom of Harvey Penick : lessons and thoughts from
the collected writings of golf's best-loved teacher /
Harvey Penick with Bud Shrake.
p.   cm.
1. Golf.   2. Golf—Anecdotes.   I. Shrake, Edwin.   II. Title.
GV965.P4143   1997
796.352—dc21   97-28126
                                CIP

ISBN 978-1-4391-6392-4

This book is written not only to help all golfers with their own games but to help club pros and teachers with their teaching.

—HARVEY PENICK,
Austin Country Club,
Austin, Texas, 1992

Contents

PART II. from *And If You Play Golf, You're My Friend* 127

THE WISDOM
OF
HARVEY PENICK

PART I

from
Harvey Penick's
Little Red Book

Introductions

---

by Tom Kite

WHETHER OR NOT you realize it, you are about to read one of the most important golf instruction books ever written, if not *the* most important. If you have never had the opportunity to take a lesson from Harvey Penick, that statement may surprise you some. But even better is the fact that this lesson will be enjoyable and you will learn something that should improve your game.

This is the effect that "Mr. Penick's son," Harvey, has had on his students for many a decade. No one can help but enjoy being around Harvey. He is as comfortable as an old pair of jeans, as unpretentious as a young child, and yet is one of the smartest men I have ever had the pleasure to meet. No, not book smart, but people smart. He truly knows, understands, and loves people. And people truly enjoy being around him. As a matter of fact, some of my favorite memories are the rainy winter days when no one was on the course and we could all gather around Harvey and try to get inside his mind.

Harvey has often said that one of the things that has helped him become a better teacher is the fact that he has probably seen more golf balls hit by more students than anyone else. But there are lots of teachers who have spent countless hours on the practice tee with students, with little in the way of results to show for it. Harvey's students always improve, and at the same time Harvey improves as a teacher. Even at this stage in his career, he says he learns something new about golf every day. Contrast that to one of today's method teachers who says there is only one way to swing the club. Harvey allows the swing to fit the student— his or her personality. What other reason could there be for the tremendous numbers of great players who have worked with Harvey while most teachers are lucky if they ever have one? There are so many tour players who have come to Austin for a checkup that any list is bound to omit some. But Mickey Wright, Betsy Rawls, Sandra Palmer, Judy Kimball, Kathy Whitworth, Terry Dill, and Don and Rik Massengale probably made the trip more than most. No less than Bob Toski once commented that only Harvey Penick could have produced two players with such different personalities and athletic abilities as Ben Crenshaw and me without stifling one while helping the other achieve greatness.

But he is not only a pro's teacher. Harvey still gets goose bumps watching a beginning student get a ball into the air for the first time or teaching a 21-handicapper to get out of a trap. For years I would have put the Austin C.C. up against any club in the nation for the number of single-digit handicappers, because if a student had some time, he or she almost had to improve with Harvey as tutor.

But don't be misled into thinking that Harvey taught us all the same thing or even the same way. I have never seen him give a group lesson. To the contrary, he would shoo away any sideline watchers for fear they would overhear something that didn't apply to their games. In over thirty years of playing golf with Ben Crenshaw, I have never been allowed to watch Ben take a lesson from Harvey, nor has he been allowed to watch me. Harvey is so careful in choosing what he says that I have often seen him fail to respond to a question until the next day for fear that his answer would be misconstrued. And I can assure you that every answer he finally did come up with was always, always expressed in a positive way. Never would Harvey say "don't do that," but "could we try a little of this?"

But when it is all said and done, when the drives no longer have the carry they used to, when the iron shots are not as crisp as they once were, and the 29 putts per round are now more like 33 or 34, the one thing that we all have learned from Harvey is love. A love of a game that teaches us more about ourselves than we sometimes care to know. And a love of the people that we share this game with. Harvey makes no distinction between the rank beginner who chops his way around the course and the touring pro with a swing as smooth as velvet. If a person loves the game, then Harvey will do anything in his power to try to help that person improve. And be assured his effect on his students is tremendous. As Dick Coop, the noted sports psychologist from the University of North Carolina, once said, "Harvey teaches in parables." I believe that Harvey must have had a good teacher too.

by Ben Crenshaw

A good friend of mine from west Texas remarked, after a lengthy conversation with me about Harvey Penick, "He seems to be the most *contented* man I have ever known." I thought that was a wonderful way to describe him. My friend, a fine player who played golf for the University of Texas, often thinks of Mr. Penick and says that Harvey's teaching philosophy, as well as his simple outlooks on life, has helped him immensely to understand how we can, after all, make the most out of life. If we only knew how good we have had it under Harvey . . .

from *Harvey Penick's Little Red Book* • 17

Tom Kite and Ben Crenshaw
with Harvey, 1985.

Golf, in any form, has given Harvey contentment. Adding to Harvey's contentment is the fact that he knew what was to be his life's work at a fairly early age. I've often wondered when Harvey met Jack Burke, Sr., who was probably the first golf professional to have a substantial influence on the improvement of early Texas golf (in the 1920s). Harvey has told me a number of times of how often many future teachers would show up at the Burke household. Burke was from Philadelphia and was most likely heavily influenced by the Scottish immigrant professionals on the Eastern Seaboard, who favored a no-nonsense fundamental approach to teaching. Of particular fascination to Harvey, I am sure, was Stewart Maiden's approach to teaching, mainly the handling of the young Bobby Jones in Atlanta. Maiden's words to his pupils were simple and direct, avoiding all technicality, which is one of Harvey's hallmarks. Harvey also said to me that the finest book of golf instruction for all is *Bobby Jones on Golf*, which contains Jones's own golfing genius as well as Maiden's, combined with miles and miles of common sense and Jones's beautiful command of the English language.

These men, along with so many other people interested in improving golf, were important in Harvey Penick's development, but what sets the great teachers apart from the others is not merely golf knowledge, but the essential art of communication. Very few teachers in golf have had it, as Harvey does, and I think that it would be safe to say that it requires a gift from Above. I know that Harvey has spent a considerable amount of his lifetime teaching golf, not thinking of *what* to say to a pupil, but *how* to say it. Harvey's messages always came across in soothing tones, for he always knew how fragile our psyches were when we were playing poorly. His mere choice of words suggested the direct antithesis of commanding tones.

For example, he would always inspect the hands of a

pupil to check for calluses. If he found them, he might say, "Let's try and *place* our hands on the club." The inference is made thus not to "grab" or "twist" or "wrap" our hands around the club. "Placing" was always a valuable word since it implies lighter grip pressure. Therefore it became easier to swing the clubhead.

In many ways Harvey reminds me of Old Tom Morris. Old Tom was a fabulous golfer from St. Andrews, Scotland, a great player who won the British Open championship four times. Old Tom was not known for his teaching ability, as Harvey is, but rather for imparting his philosophies and the tradition of the game of golf to others in a way that stirred deep emotions. As Honorary Professional and Custodian of the Links at St. Andrews, he had seen many changes in the game, and this beloved character lived a long and prosperous life knowing that he contributed to others' enjoyment of the game, regardless of their level of achievement. Old Tom was wise, treated all men equally, and kept things very simple. It did not take much to make him happy. As long as he was around his many friends, and there was golf to be played and talked about, he was truly *contented.* Many times Old Tom would say "I've got mae God and mae gowff to see me thro'."

What a joy it will be for people who are serious about their game to read about Harvey Penick's life of helping others. The golf parts are easily understandable as they contain such a simple, common sense style. But those of us who are lucky enough to have been around him for a while have truly been touched by a man with unfailing courtesy and generosity, a special kindness the likes of which I have never before witnessed in any man. I have never, ever heard of him remotely raising his voice to another; he is truly a man filled with compassion for others. For all of his admirable traits, let us simply say that Harvey Penick represents the very best that life and golf can offer.

by Betsy Rawls

Harvey Penick was my only golf teacher for thirty years, until I retired from competitive golf in 1975. For me, Harvey reduced golf, as he did life, to a few sound, irrefutable, worthwhile principles. And he expressed those principles in simple unadorned, down-to-earth, and often humorous terms.

He was always a refuge from the complexities and emotional traumas of the tour. To come back and see Harvey was to become refreshed, to become inspired, and to be able to put things in perspective once more.

He always brought me back to the basic mechanics on which a good swing is built.

Harvey's strength of character, his morals, his dedication, and his great wisdom somehow made me a stronger and wiser person. To have had Harvey as a teacher, a mentor, and a friend has been one of the great blessings of my life.

by Mickey Wright

I had the pleasure of spending quite a few hours on the practice tee of the Austin Country Club with Harvey Penick, not only having him look at my swing but watching and listening to him.

I was always struck by the simplicity of his teaching. He insisted on a good grip as a prime determinant of the swing and tried to impart to his students the feel of a good swing through various devices he would have them swing, such as a scythe or a heavy ball on a chain.

He worked with his difficult students as individuals and didn't try to fit them into a mold. He stressed, appropriately, a good short game, and his outstanding students, like Ben Crenshaw, Tom Kite, and Kathy Whitworth, were certainly outstanding in this area.

by Kathy Whitworth

Harvey Penick is not only the consummate club and teaching professional but a unique individual. He has never been interested in the financial rewards or the publicity that may have come his way. I personally do not remember ever paying for a lesson after the first few visits.

His biggest reward, he told me, was to help someone hit the ball better than they ever hit it before. His demeanor, his honesty, his integrity in how he lives his everyday life have probably had as much of an impact on me as his teaching. To try to live up to his standards has been a wonderful experience and will be even more so since I am now trying to become a teaching professional myself.

Harvey has touched many lives through the years, and with this book and through the people who have had the privilege to know him, he will continue to touch many more. What a nice thought.

My Little Red Book

AN OLD PRO told me that originality does not consist of saying what has never been said before; it consists of saying what you have to say that you know to be the truth.

Harvey with his original
little red book, 1994.

More than sixty years ago, I began writing notes and observations in what I came to call my Little Red Book. Until recently I had never let anyone read my Little Red Book except my son, Tinsley. My wife, Helen, could have read it, of course, but a lifetime spent living with a grown-up caddie like me provided Helen with all the information about golf that she cares to know.

My intention was to pass my Little Red Book on to Tinsley, who is the head professional at Austin Country Club. Tinsley was named to that post in 1973, when I retired with the title of Head Professional Emeritus after holding the job for fifty years.

With the knowledge in this little book to use as a reference, it would be easier for Tinsley to make a good living teaching golf no matter what happens when I am gone.

Tinsley is a wonderful teacher on his own and has added insights to this book over the years. But there is only one copy of the red Scribbletex notebook that I wrote in. I kept it locked in my briefcase. Most of my club members and the players who came to me for help heard about my Little Red Book as it slowly grew into what is still a slender volume considering that all the important truths I have learned about golf are written in its pages.

Many asked to read the book. I wouldn't show it to Tommy Kite, Ben Crenshaw, Betsy Rawls, Kathy Whitworth, Betty Jameson, Sandra Palmer, or any of the others, no matter how much I loved them.

What made my Little Red Book special was not that what was written in it had never been said before. It was that what it says about playing golf has stood the test of time.

I see things written about the golf swing that I can't believe will work except by accident. But whether it is for beginners, medium players, experts, or children, anything I say in my book has been tried and tested with success.

One morning last spring I was sitting in my golf cart under the trees on the grass near the veranda at Austin Country Club. I was with my nurse, Penny, a patient young woman who drives us in my golf cart a few blocks from home to the club on days when I feel well enough for the journey.

I don't stay more than an hour or two on each visit, and I don't go more than three or four times a week because I don't want the members to think of me as a ghost that refuses to go away.

I don't want to cut into the teaching time of any of our fine club professionals, either. I can see Jackson Bradley out teaching on the practice line, and there are moments when I might want to make a suggestion, but I don't do it.

However, I can't refuse to help when my old friend Tommy Kite, the leading money winner in the history of the game, walks over to my golf cart and asks if I will watch him putt for a while. Tommy asks almost shyly, as if afraid I might not feel strong enough. His request makes my heart leap with joy.

I spend nights staring at the ceiling, thinking of what I have seen Tommy doing in tournaments on television, and praying that he will come see me. If Tommy wants, I will break my rule that I never visit the club on weekends, and will have Penny drive me to the putting green to meet with Tommy on Saturday and Sunday morning, as well as on Thursday and Friday. I know it exasperates Penny that I would rather watch Tommy putt than eat the lunch she has to force on me.

Or I may be sitting in my cart in the shade enjoying the spring breeze and the rolling greenery of our beautiful golf course, with the blue water of Lake Austin sparkling below, as good and peaceful a place as I know on this earth, and the young touring pro Cindy Figg-Currier may stop and say hello and eventually work up the nerve to ask if I will look at her putting stroke.

Certainly I will. I get as much pleasure out of helping a rising young pro like Cindy as I do a celebrated hero like Tommy.

Don Massengale of the Senior Tour had phoned me at home the night before for a long-distance putting lesson. I can't hear very well on the phone, and Helen had to interpret, shouting back and forth as I tried to straighten out Don's grip.

Earlier my old friend Ben Crenshaw, the Masters champion who had grown up with Tommy Kite in the group of boys that I taught at the old Austin Country Club across town, dropped by our home for a visit and brought his wife and daughter to see Helen and me. Ben is one of the greatest players of all time, a natural. When he was a boy I wouldn't let him practice too much for fear that he might find out how to do something wrong. Ben has his own course, designed by Ben and his partner, at the Barton Creek Country Club layout, a ten-minute drive away from us. It pleases me deeply when Ben drops by to sit on the couch or when he phones me from some tournament.

Ben hasn't been gone long before the doorbell rings and it's one of our members, Gil Kuykendall, who brings Air Force General Robin Olds into the living room and asks if I will give the general a lesson on the rug from my wheelchair. They are entered in a tournament, and the general has played golf only a few times. Can I teach him? In the living room? In half an hour?

General Olds is a jolly good fellow, thick through the chest. He was a football star at West Point. He has those big muscles that, as Bobby Jones said, can bend a bar but are no use in swinging a golf club.

I fit the general with a strong grip and teach him a very short swing. Just about waist high to waist high. This man is too muscle-bound to make a full swing, but he is strong enough to advance the ball decently with a short swing. He may not break 100 in the tournament, but he will make it around the golf course.

When the member and the general leave, Helen and Penny scold me. I am wearing myself out, they say. They remind me that before Ben dropped by, a girl who is hoping to make the University of Texas team had come to talk to me about her progress, and I had asked questions for an hour.

It's true that I have grown tired as the day became evening. But my mind is excited. My heart is thrilled. I have been teaching. Nothing has ever given me greater pleasure than teaching. I received as much joy from coaxing a first-time pupil, a woman from Paris, into hitting the ball into the air so that she could go back to France and play golf with her husband as I did from watching the development of all the fine players I have been lucky enough to know.

When one of my less talented pupils would, under my guidance, hit a first-class shot, I would say, "I hope that gives you as much pleasure as it does me." I would get goose pimples on my arms and a prickly feeling on my neck from the joy of being able to help.

Every time I found something about the swing or the stance or the mental approach that proved to be consistently successful, I wrote it down in my Little Red Book.

Occasionally I added impressions of champions I have known, from Walter Hagen and Bobby Jones to Ben Hogan, Byron Nelson, and Sam Snead to Jack Nicklaus and Arnold Palmer to Kite and Crenshaw, as well as Rawls, Whitworth, Jameson, Mickey Wright, Sandra Palmer, and many other distinguished players.

I prefer to teach with images, parables, and metaphors that plant in the mind the seeds of shotmaking. These, too, went into the notebook—if they proved successful.

Many professional writers inquired during my long career as a teacher if they might write a book for me on how to play golf.

I always politely declined. For one thing, I never regarded myself as any kind of genius. I was a humble student and teacher of the game. What I was learning was not for the purpose of promoting myself in the public eye. I was never interested in money. What I was learning was to be shared only with my pupils, and ultimately the knowledge would belong to my son, Tinsley, and my daughter, Kathryn.

But on this soft spring morning that I mentioned earlier, with squirrels playing in the grass around the wheels of my cart, and a shiny black grackle prowling in the branches above me, I was sitting there wondering if I was being selfish.

Maybe it was wrong to hoard the knowledge I had accumulated. Maybe I had been granted these eighty-seven years of life and this wonderful career in order that I should pass on to everyone what I had learned. This gift had not been given me to keep secret.

A writer, Bud Shrake, who lives in the hills near the club, came to visit with me under the trees on this particular morning.

Penny gave Bud her seat in my cart. We chatted a few minutes about his brother, Bruce, who was one of my boys during the thirty-three years I was the golf coach at the University of Texas. Then it burst out of me.

"I want to show you something that nobody except Tinsley has ever read," I said.

I unlocked my briefcase and handed him my Little Red Book.

I asked if he might help me get it in shape to be published.

Bud went into the golf shop and brought Tinsley out to my cart.

I asked Tinsley if he thought we should share our book with a larger crowd than the two of us.

Tinsley had a big grin on his face.

"I've been waiting and hoping for you to say that," he said.

So that morning under the trees we opened my Little Red Book.

Golf Medicine

WHEN I ASK YOU to take an aspirin, please don't take the whole bottle.

In the golf swing a tiny change can make a huge difference. The natural inclination is to begin to overdo the tiny change that has brought success. So you exaggerate in an effort to improve even more, and soon you are lost and confused again.

Lessons are not to take the place of practice but to make practice worthwhile.

Looking Up

LOOKING UP IS the biggest alibi ever invented to explain a terrible shot.

By the time you look up, you've already made the mistake that caused the bad shot.

When I tell a student to keep his eye on the ball, it is usually to give him something to think about that won't do any harm.

I've known only three or four top players who say they actually see the ball when they hit it. Even Ben Hogan told me he loses sight of the ball "somewhere in my downswing."

Hand Position

I LIKE TO see your hands toward the inside of your left thigh on every shot except the driver.

With the driver, I like to see your hands at your zipper. If this moves them slightly behind the ball at address, that is fine. It encourages hitting on the upswing.

The Three Most Important Clubs

HERBERT WARREN WIND, the stylish and learned golf writer, came to see me at the club and asked what I think are the three most important clubs in the bag, in order.

I said, "The putter, the driver, and the wedge."

Herb said he'd asked Ben Hogan the same question. Ben had replied, "The driver, the putter, and the wedge."

My reasoning is that you hit the driver fourteen times in an ordinary round. But on the same day, you may have 23–25 putts that are outside the "gimme" range but within a makable distance.

A five-foot putt counts one stroke, the same as a 270-yard drive, but the putt may be much more significant to your score.

Psychologically, the driver is very important. If you hit your tee ball well, it fills you with confidence. On the other hand, if you smash a couple of drives into the trees, your confidence can be shaken.

But nothing is more important psychologically than knocking putts into the hole. Sinking putts makes your confidence soar, and it devastates your opponent.

A good putter is a match for anyone. A bad putter is a match for no one.

The woods are full of long drivers.

The Grip

IF YOU HAVE a bad grip, you don't want a good swing.

With a bad grip you have to make unattractive adjustments in your swing to hit the ball squarely.

It's no good to make a beautiful Al Geiberger swing unless you grip the club like he does. If Al twisted his hands around into some kind of ugly grip and then made his graceful swing, he might knock the ball out of bounds.

I believe it is a nice idea to try to pattern your swing after that of a professional player who is close to your own height and body structure, but only if you also study and imitate that player's grip.

As a teacher I have learned that one of the most delicate matters to attend to is the student's grip.

If the student comes to me as a once-a-week player who has been playing for years without improving, all I have to do is put his hands on the club in a good grip—and after the lesson I will never see him again. He will hit the ball so poorly that he will think I am the dumbest teacher in the country.

Changing a bad grip into a good grip requires a great amount of practice. Unless the student is willing and able to do this, I would indeed be a dumb teacher if I demanded a radical alteration from an ordinary player in one lesson.

But with a talented player who plays and practices often, it can be a different, almost miraculous story.

Kirby Attwell was trying to make my team at the University of Texas. He had a good swing but a weak grip that caused an open clubface. His shots lacked authority and mostly flew off to the right of the target, except when he would try so hard to square the clubface that he would hit a nasty hook.

After I knew the boy and his game well enough, I moved his left hand to the right. Then I moved his right hand a bit more to the right, also.

Don't think that because you move your left hand you must automatically move the right to make it match. Often it's enough to move one hand and leave the other alone. But in this boy's case, he needed a stronger grip all around.

Kirby looked at his hands as I placed them on the club, and there was an expression of disbelief on his face.

"Harvey," he said, "if I hit the ball with this grip, I'll hook it over the fence."

Harvey, 1925.

I asked him to try.

He cracked a long, powerful shot that went as straight as a ball can go. He was astonished and delighted. Kirby became an excellent player at the University of Texas. But he had talent and the time and desire to take his new grip to the practice range and become confident with it before he took it to the golf course.

One grip does not fit all.

The interlocking grip, with the forefinger of the top hand laced between the little finger and the ring finger of the bottom hand, is for people who have short fingers. Gene Sarazen, Jack Nicklaus, and Tom Kite use it.

The overlapping grip, with the little finger of the bottom hand wrapped into the hollow between the forefinger and middle finger of the top hand or on top of the left forefinger, is the most widely used among ordinary players as well as experts, though with many individual variations. Ben Hogan, Arnold Palmer, Byron Nelson, Ben Crenshaw, Sam Snead, Al Geiberger, and Payne Stewart are just a few of the overlappers, and none of their grips are exactly alike.

The two-hand or ten-finger grip, with all the fingers on the handle—sometimes called the baseball grip (although the baseball bat is held more in the palms, and a golf club more in the fingers)—is especially good for women and older players who may lack strength, although some top professionals like Beth Daniel, Art Wall, and Bob Rosburg have done well with it. Little Alice Ritzman adopted the ten-finger grip as my student and gained enough distance to play on the tour and become one of the longer drivers.

In his famous book, *Five Lessons,* written with Herb Wind, Hogan says the tips of the thumb and forefinger of the bottom hand should never touch each other. Others teach that the thumb and forefinger should meld like a trigger. Bobby Jones used the overlapping grip with the tip of his right forefinger not touching the handle at all. But the back of the first joint of his forefinger pressed against the handle. Victor East of Spalding built special grips with flat places for the back of Jones's right forefinger, which would be illegal today.

I can go on and on talking about the grip until it gets too deep for me to understand.

The fact is, a top player can change his grip enough to cause a draw or a fade, a slice or a hook, and an observer can't even see the change. The top player feels it; and it happens.

I happen to have long fingers, and long fingers feel good on a club in the overlapping grip.

If you will pick up a yardstick and let your hands fit it, that will come closer to giving you a good grip than anything I could write about where to point your V's and all of that.

Just pick up a yardstick and fit your hands to it and swing it.

Then put the same grip on a golf club.

There is one thing I like to see in common with all three grips. I don't want the left thumb straight down the top of the handle. I want the thumb a little bit to the right. Byron Nelson told me the left thumb position is one of the most important things I teach. The reason is that at the top of the backswing, that thumb wants to be underneath the club. This gives you control.

Coaching at the University of Texas, I encountered a lot of west Texas boys. West Texas boys were well known for their strong grips, which they develop because they play in the wind so often. They can hit a 7-iron so far you can't believe it. Off the tee they get great distances with a 3-wood or 4-wood, but they can't hit a driver Their strong grips delofted the clubs so much that a driver face would be totally shut.

Billy Maxwell was the first west Texas boy I can remember who had what I would call a good grip, with his hands more on top of the club.

No matter which of the three grips you use, one fundamental is that the hands must be touching each other. They should be joined as one unit. They should feel like they are melted together.

The best thing to do is to find a grip that fits you and feels good and then stay with it.

If the ball is flying pretty well, your grip is all right.

If you keep fooling with your grip, you will find yourself making a mistake on your backswing to correct for your new grip and then making another mistake on your downswing to correct the mistake you made on your backswing.

As for your grip pressure, keep it light.

Arnold Palmer likes to grip the club tightly, but you are not Arnold Palmer.

The Waggle

I THINK THE MAIN value of the waggle is that it turns on your juice and gets your adrenaline flowing.

The waggle is also a small practice swing and a way to ease tension, unless you get so involved in waggling you forget your purpose.

One of my club players took twenty-one waggles before he could swing the club. People in his foursome would look the other way when it was his turn to hit.

Ben Hogan has a solid piece of advice: Don't groove your waggle. Just get the feel and swing. Bobby Jones said if you saw him waggle more than twice, he probably hit a bad shot.

I don't like to see a player waggle up and down. To me it looks amateurish.

The great Horton Smith used no waggle at all.

Holding the Club

THERE IS AN ARTFULNESS to holding the club that goes beyond the craft of gripping it. I was teaching at a seminar in New York and, as usual, holding a club. Not that I thought I was Bob Hope, but I always found it much easier to talk to people, especially large groups, if I had a golf club in my hands.

I heard one of the pros say, "Look at Harvey. He holds that club like it's a fine musical instrument."

That's how a golf club feels to me: like a fine musical instrument.

At another seminar in Houston, Jackson Bradley, Jimmy Demaret, Jack Burke, Jr., and I were teaching, and I pointed out how beautifully Jackie Burke held the club. His hands looked perfectly natural.

"Let me add," Jackson Bradley said, "that Jackie's hands look perfect, but so do his clothes." Jackson showed us his own hands. "My fingers are a little crooked. My grip may be just as good as Jackie's, but my hands will never look as good on a club as his do."

Look at the club in the hands of Ben Crenshaw. His hands and fingers fit so gracefully, so naturally, that I am moved to regard his grip as a piece of art.

The same can be said for Mickey Wright and Dave Marr, among others.

Tommy Kite and Jack Nicklaus have a good grip on the club, but they will never look as artful because their fingers are short and they use the interlocking grip which is not as appealing to my eyes.

The Easiest Lesson

THE EASIEST GOLF lesson I ever gave was to Don January.

Don had been a star player at North Texas State University and a winner on the Texas amateur circuit, a regular round of tournaments that drew so many championship-quality golfers that I could fill up a whole book with their names.

Now Don was wondering if he could make it on the professional tour. He came to see me and asked if I would take a look at his swing and tell him my honest opinion of his game and help correct any flaws.

I watched Don hit a few putts. We went to the practice range. I asked him to hit a half-dozen short irons for me. Then I asked him to hit a half-dozen middle irons, followed by several long irons.

I could tell he was waiting for me to say something.

Instead I asked him to hit a few drives.

When he had done so, he turned and said, "Well? What do I need?"

I said, "Don, you need to pack your clubs and go to California and join the tour."

End of lesson.

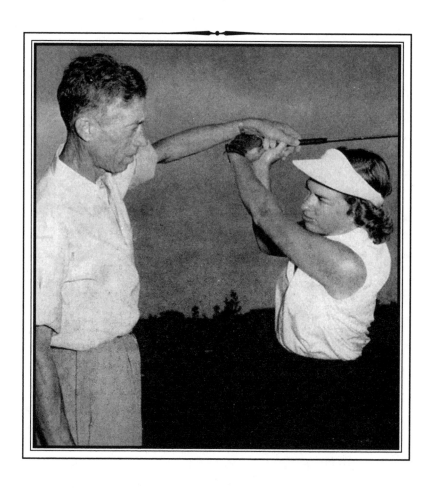

Harvey with Betsy Rawls, 1954.

Palm Reading

PEOPLE ARE ALWAYS asking me to look at the calluses on their palms, as if the location and thickness of the calluses will tell me whether their grip is correct.

I remember someone asking to see the calluses on Sam Snead's palms. Sam said, "I don't have any calluses." Sam said he holds the club as if it is a live bird in his hands, with just enough pressure that the bird can't fly away but not so tightly that the bird can't breathe. Grip the club this way and you won't have calluses, either.

Hold onto the club firmly but not tightly, with your elbows and shoulders slightly relaxed. This is especially important for women. It helps them to hit with more snap.

Where the calluses come from is a player putting his hands on the club and then twisting them into what looks like a good grip when in fact it is not a good grip.

Place your hands on the club correctly and leave them alone. There's no need to screw them around in a vain effort to make your V's point where you think they should point.

If you insist on moving your hands and fingers after taking your grip, you accomplish two things that you do not want: You camouflage a poor grip; and you get calluses.

Starting Young

THE BEST AGE to start a child in golf is the time he or she becomes interested in the game.

I don't believe in parents forcing the game on kids who would rather be doing something else. But if a little child four or five years old is eager to go out and play with Dad or Mom, then it's time to start.

Don't be too exacting on the grip or anything else. Just let the kids use their natural ability. Hands together.

Be sure the club you give them has plenty of loft. Problems start when the child uses too little loft and tries to scoop the ball up into the air. The more the child tries to help the ball up, the less it'll get up.

Also be sure the club is light enough. A small child will learn a bad grip by trying to swing a club that is too heavy. My cousin, Dr. D. A. Penick, a professor of Greek who rode around town on a bicycle and was the tennis coach at the University of Texas for fifty years, discouraged toddlers from swinging a tennis racquet for that same reason.

When you take your youngster to see a teaching pro, say that you're going to get some "help." The word "lessons" sounds too much like going to school, which is not always fun. Golf should be fun. With a child I never say "teach" or "lessons."

Group instruction for kids is all right, but in some cases the teaching can be overcomplicated to the point where it interferes with the child's natural ability. Beware especially the group instructor who is a poor player and teaches the kids what he has just read in the latest how-to-hit-it book, which the instructor may not even understand.

If you see an instructor trying to teach a whole group of kids to imitate the stance and swing of Ben Hogan, for example, take your child out of that group. The way Hogan does it is special to Hogan. Your child is special in his or her own way.

A professional should look at the child's swing maybe once a month, just to steer the game on the right track. No more.

Practicing is an individual matter. When they were kids, Ben Crenshaw was always playing more than he practiced, and Tom Kite was always practicing at least as much as he played. Hogan was a practicer. Byron Nelson was a player and also a practicer.

Whatever the child wants to do—play or practice—that's what he or she should do.

Worst of all is when I see Dad, on the range or the course, constantly nagging the child to keep his head down, keep his left arm straight, stare at the ball—bad information, all of it. This may be fun for Dad, but it is hurting the child's development.

If you are fortunate enough to be able to give your child plenty of free time to spend at a golf course, and the right amount of help from a professional teacher, your child will be beating you sooner than you may think.

Hole Them All

TWO PROUD PARENTS came to me at the club and announced that their young son had just scored his first birdie.

I agreed that was a wonderful event and asked them how long was the putt Junior made for the birdie

The parents said the putt was only two feet long, so they gave Junior a "gimme" to assure his first birdie.

"I've got bad news for you," I said. "Junior still hasn't made his first birdie."

Not only did Junior not sink the birdie putt, it was now planted in his mind that he could pick up his ball two feet from the hole and pronounce the putt as made, not having to face the moment of truth

When Junior reaches a higher level of play, where there are no "gimmes," he may develop an anxiety about short putts that will bother him the rest of his life.

My rule is that a youngster, no matter how small, should be required to hole every putt.

If Junior grows up knowing he has to make all the short ones, that will automatically become part of his game. When he plays on higher levels and faces a two-footer to win an important match, he'll be ready.

Learning Around the Cup

GOLF SHOULD BE learned starting at the cup and progressing back toward the tee.

I'm talking about with children. The same thing applies to adult beginners, but adults think that is too simple. An adult beginner—especially a man—thinks he's not getting his money's worth if you ask him to spend an hour sinking short putts. He wants to pull out his driver and smack it, which is the very last thing he will learn if he comes to me.

If a beginner tries to learn the game at the tee and move on toward the green, postponing the short game until last, this is one beginner who will be lucky ever to beat anybody.

What I like to see is a youngster learning the game on the practice green with one chipping club, a putter, and one golf ball.

A chipping stroke is just a short version of a full swing.

A child will learn a good chipping stroke and the unteachable qualities of touch and feel if the grown-ups will let it happen.

The best stroke in the world is not much good without touch or feel. An individual-looking stroke that the child has confidence in and a feel for how to use, and that puts the ball close to the hole, is the best stroke in the world for that child.

I will take a chipper and putter who has touch any time over someone who has a beautiful stroke but no sense of feel for where the ball is going to roll.

Many of the best putters and chippers in history learned in the caddie yard.

I like for a child to use one ball, chip it at the hole, and then go put it in. This is how the child learns to score.

For a child to chip a dozen or more balls at the same hole, one after the other, is a poor method. It gives too much room for mistakes. If a child can hit a bad chip and then just drag over another ball and hit it again, it does not teach the reality of playing golf, which is that you have to pay for your mistakes.

The best thing is for the child to play games with other children on and around the practice green. I like for them to play each other for something, whether it's matchsticks or a soda pop or an imaginary U.S. Open championship—just as long as there is something at stake that makes the child concentrate on getting his or her ball into the cup in fewer strokes than the other kids. Some children are natural competitors at golf, some must learn to be, and some couldn't care less. Playing games sharpens or teaches competition. Those who don't care will drift into something else that they do care about.

I remember when Ben Crenshaw was six years old, two years before he took his first lesson from me, he and his daddy Charlie and the great tennis player Wilmer Allison, who succeeded my cousin as tennis coach at Texas, would go around and around and around the putting green, hour after hour. Ben was developing the touch and stroke that made him one of the finest putters in history. It wasn't long before he was winning quarters from the grown-ups.

Not everyone agrees with me on learning the game from the cup backward, of course.

Arnold Palmer's daddy taught him to hit the ball hard at a very young age. There was a shot at their golf course that called for a long carry over water. Young Arnold would stand there and bet the grown-ups coming through a dime or a quarter that he could hit it over the water—and he could. At the same time, Arnold became a top putter.

That's the thing about golf. Outside of the USGA rule book, there are no indisputable ways the game must be learned or played.

But if your child will learn to play on and around the green first of all, I am convinced that in most cases progress will be more rapid and the skills will be longer-lasting.

Do You Need Help?

IF YOU PLAY poorly one day, forget it.

If you play poorly the next time out, review your fundamentals of grip, stance, aim, and ball position. Most mistakes are made before the club is swung.

If you play poorly for a third time in a row, go see your professional.

Take Dead Aim

WHEN MY STUDENT Betsy Rawls was in a playoff for the U.S. Women's Open championship, I sent her a one-sentence telegram.

It said: "Take dead aim!"

Betsy won the playoff.

For golfers who might not understand Texas talk, let me put the advice in the telegram a different way: Once you address the golf ball, hitting it has got to be the most important thing in your life at that moment. Shut out all thoughts other than picking out a target and taking dead aim at it.

This is a good way to calm a case of nerves.

Everybody gets nervous on the first tee, whether it's Betsy Rawls in a playoff for the Open or a high handicapper teeing off at the club in a two-dollar Nassau with pals.

Instead of worrying about making a fool of yourself in front of a crowd of 4 or 40,000, forget about how your swing may look and concentrate instead on where you want the ball to go. Pretty is as pretty does.

I would approach my college players before a match and tell them the same thing: Take dead aim.

This is a wonderful thought to keep in mind all the way around the course, not just on the first tee. Take dead aim at a spot on the fairway or the green, refuse to allow any negative thought to enter your head, and swing away.

A high handicapper will be surprised at how often the mind will make the muscles hit the ball to the target, even with a far less than perfect swing.

The expert player won't be surprised. The expert expects to hit the target. The only surprise here is that the expert sometimes allows disorganized thinking to make him or her become distracted from the primary object of the shot, which is to hit the target.

I can't say it too many times. It's the most important advice in this book.

Take dead aim.

Make it a point to do it every time on every shot. Don't just do it from time to time, when you happen to remember.

Take dead aim.

Beware

ONE OF MY University of Texas golfers was playing in a tournament in North Carolina. He won his first match handily.

He phoned me and said, "The guy I play tomorrow I can beat easily. He has a bad grip and also a bad swing."

My boy lost the next match.

"The lesson to be learned," I told my golfer later, "is don't be afraid of the player with a good grip and a bad swing. Don't be afraid of a player with a bad grip and a good swing. The player to beware of is the one with the bad grip and the bad swing. If he's reached your level, he has grooved his faults and knows how to score."

How to Knock Five Strokes Off Your Game

THE AVERAGE GOLFER does not improve stroke by stroke.

Improvement comes in plateaus.

A player who shoots 95 does not through lessons and practice see his or her score drop slowly to 94, then 93, then 92, 91, 90. Nor does the 87-shooter come down gradually to 86, 85, 84.

Instead the 95 suddenly falls to 90. The 87 will seemingly overnight become an 81.

By the same token, a player who regularly shoots 80 can quickly fall into the middle 70s. Once you reach 75 or so, you are no longer an average golfer but are approaching the expert level, where improvement comes more slowly.

But even some 75-shooters can reach a mini-plateau and see their scores go down by three shots or so after a week of practice.

There can be many reasons why the 95 becomes a 90. Maybe the player learns to cure his slice. The 87 may become an 81 because the player learns to hit the ball twenty yards farther off the tee and now can reach more greens in regulation.

As a general rule, however, the 75-shooter can become a 72-shooter only if he improves his short game—unless it was his short-game wizardry that made him shoot 75 in the first place.

The short game. Those are the magic words.

The higher your score, the faster you can lower it—with the short game.

There's no mystery to it. Anybody who plays much golf knows that about half of his shots are struck within sixty yards of the flagstick.

And yet when I see an average golfer practicing, where is he? Most likely he is on the range, banging away with his driver.

If I ask an average golfer what percentage of his practice time he spends on his short game in comparison to hitting the longer shots, he'll probably tell me he gives the short game 10 or 20 percent. This is usually a fib. The average golfer will devote fifteen minutes to stroking a few putts if he has time before he heads for the first tee, and that's about it for the short-game practice.

Well, if you want to see a radical improvement in your game and cut off five strokes in a week or two, you must make a radical change in the way you practice.

For two weeks devote 90 percent of your practice time to chipping and putting, and only 10 percent to the full swing. If you do this, your 95 will turn into 90. I guarantee it.

I can see the average player nodding his head and saying yeah, yeah. I know that's what I ought to do.

But I don't see him doing it.

Instead I see him on the range, swinging from the heels, hitting forty drives in a row for the thrill of those four or five that might be well struck.

I would never let my college players or the touring pros who come to me for help hit forty driver shots in a row. This causes fatigue and very bad habits.

My college players and touring pros, being experts, understand the immense importance of the short game. Tom Kite, for example, puts in many hours on his full swing, but he practices his wedges and his chipping and putting even more because he knows that's what causes good scores, and without good scores he wouldn't be the all-time leading money winner in golf.

So if you want to knock five shots off your game in a hurry, leave your long clubs in your bag and head for the green.

Bobby Jones said the secret of shooting low scores is the ability to turn three shots into two.

It reminds me of a college match I saw. I had a good player named Billy Munn, who was matched against R. H. Sikes of Arkansas at the old Austin Country Club.

Billy hit every fairway and seventeen greens and shot 67. Sikes hit few fairways and maybe five greens. But Sikes shot 66 and beat Billy 1-up.

After the match I found Billy and said, "I'm very proud of you. You played a wonderful round of golf. But, Billy, don't ever think what you saw out there today was luck."

Sikes had a great short game, as he went on to prove on the professional tour.

You may never develop a short game to equal Sikes's, but if you practice hard on chipping and putting you can bring your score down fast. It's all up to you.

Emerson said, "Thinking is the hardest work in the world. That's why so few of us do it."

Too many golfers think chipping and putting is hard work. That's why so few of them do it.

Reassurance

ONE OF MY favorite students, Sandra Palmer, a very successful player on the LPGA Tour, phoned me one night from the site of the U.S. Women's Open.

Sandra was worried about the speed of the greens. She said they were the slickest, fastest greens she had ever seen. The tournament started the next morning, and Sandra was getting the jitters wondering if she could putt greens like this. Should she try to change her stroke?

I knew Sandra was a fine putter and what she needed was reassurance.

"Well, Sandra," I said, "if the greens are that fast, you probably should hit your putts a little easier."

That's all it took.

Students are always asking if they should switch to heavier putters when they go play at a club with faster greens. It's probably true that if you went through the members' bags at Oakmont—famous for its fast greens—you would find heavy putters in most of them. But you should stick with your favorite putter when you go to a course with faster (or slower) greens. It's easier to get the feel or different greens than for a different putter.

The Practice Swing

HOW MANY TIMES have you seen an average golfer take two or three beautiful practice swings and then step up to the ball and make a swing that is totally different and causes an ugly shot?

It happens over and over.

As a caddie, a pro, a teacher, and starter at the first tee over the past seventy-five years, I have probably seen more golf swings than any person alive. The practice swing and real swing I just described, I must have seen a million times.

And what does the average golfer say? "If I could just hit the ball with my practice swing, I'd be a terrific player."

The reason he doesn't hit the ball with his practice swing is simple: With his practice swing he doesn't have to square his clubface on impact. He allows himself to swing freely. When there's a golf ball in front of him, he knows—at least subconsciously—that he must square that clubface, and tension sets in, causing all sorts of faults.

Now let me ask another question: How many times have you seen a player make two or three beautiful practice swings that don't touch anything but air?

These swings are useful for loosening up, but they are no good when it comes to hitting the ball.

From now on when you take a practice swing, make it a point to aim at something. Cut off a dandelion or a blade of grass, or if you are in your living room aim at a spot on the rug (but please don't take a divot and tell your wife Harvey made you do it).

Aiming at something with your practice swing will help you learn to square the clubface. Never take another practice swing without aiming it at something.

One more thing about practice swings.

Taking two or three practice swings before every shot when you are on the course playing golf takes up too much time. In these days of the four- or five-hour round, we need to speed up the game, not slow it down

At many courses in Scotland and England there is a sign on the first tee that says, "A round of golf requires no more than 3 hours, 15 minutes. If you are on the course longer than this, a marshal will come escort you off."

You don't see those Scots loitering in the fairway to take practice swings.

The Average Golfer

I USE THE TERM "average golfer" a lot, but sometimes I wonder, what is an average golfer?

I read somewhere that statistics show the average male golfer shoots about 92.

I don't believe it. Not if he counts every stroke and plays by USGA rules. Playing our Pete Dye course from the men's tees and holing every shot, the average golfer won't break 100.

A party of four Japanese gentlemen once showed up as special guests to play our course, which they had heard about in Tokyo.

I asked how well they played so I would know which of our four sets of tees—women's, seniors', men's, or championship—I would suggest.

They said they were average players and would use the championship tees because they wanted to see the whole course.

Well, I knew they wouldn't see the whole course from the back tees, because they couldn't hit the ball over our canyons from back there. But they were guests.

It took them twenty minutes and three lost balls to get past our first hole, which is relatively easy—a sharp dogleg left uphill over a ravine. About six hours later, I realized our Japanese gentlemen were still on the course, and I went to find them.

They were on the fourteenth hole. One was off in the trees, another was down in a canyon, the third was searching in the deep rough on a hillside, and the fourth greeted me with a smile.

"Very good course," he said.

"How are you doing?" I asked.

"Very good," he said.

Dick Metz said a club pro is half-mule and half-slave. Instead of escorting them off the course, I politely urged them to try to finish before dark, and then I went back to the clubhouse.

Later I heard them figuring up their scores. Every one of them shot in the low 90s.

The fact is, by USGA rules not a one of them broke 100—on the first nine.

But of course they weren't really average golfers, either.

How to Tell
Where You're Aimed

TAKE YOUR STANCE and hold a clubshaft along the front of your *thighs*. Look where the club is pointing, and you will see where you are aimed.

Laying a club on the ground at your feet will tell you very little.

Much is made of how to aim.

Hit the ball solidly, and I can show you where you were aimed. Once you learn this, your mind will tell you how to aim.

Seasoned Citizens

ONE OF THE MANY wonderful things about golf is that it is a game you can play for the rest of your life.

In fact, Seasoned Citizens—a term I much prefer to "Senior"—may get even more enjoyment out of the game than they did when they were young, because the deeper you get into golf, the more you learn to value the freedom, the companionship, the joy of being outdoors in beautiful surroundings, and the profound mysteries of the game itself.

From the family album:
Harvey with son Tinsley on
the running board, 1934.

with Kathryn Lee, 1936.

Above: with Helen, Tinsley, and
Kathryn Lee at the beach, 1946.

Left: with Kathryn Lee
and Tinsley, 1938.

Like chess, golf is a game that is forever challenging but can never be conquered.

As a golfer grows older and becomes a Seasoned Citizen, age does take its toll on the eyesight, the muscles, the flexibility, and all too often on the waistline.

But there are many ways a Seasoned Citizen can continue to score as well as when young, or perhaps score better due to the wisdom of age and the new equipment that is available.

First and foremost, a Seasoned Citizen must make every effort to maintain good physical condition.

If you can walk the golf course, do it. Get out of that golf cart. If your companions in your regular foursome insist on riding, it's all right to go along with them, but you should hop out of the cart and walk at every opportunity.

Carry two or three clubs in hand that you know you may need, and don't be afraid of slowing your companions down. The truth is that a briskly walking foursome will usually go around the course faster than a foursome in golf carts.

Golfers in carts are always driving here and there from one ball to the other, taking up a lot of time. If a rule is in effect that the cart is not allowed to leave the path, golfers are inclined to dawdle over club selection and make unnecessary trips back and forth from the ball to the bag.

Carts are very valuable tools for Seasoned Citizens who can't physically go around the course without them. One of our members is hooked up to an oxygen tank, but the golf cart allows him to continue to enjoy playing the game.

I've noticed that walkers tend to band together. If you walk and either carry a lightweight bag or pull your clubs on a trolley, you'll soon find a regular game with like-minded players.

Walking keeps a Seasoned Citizen's legs strong, and strong legs make for a more powerful swing.

I will stress here—and this is vital—that a Seasoned Citizen must let the left heel come off the ground in the backswing.

Let the left heel come up and the left arm bend for a longer, freer swing.

Some modern teachers demand that their students keep the left heel on the ground. I don't agree with that teaching for players of any age, but especially not for a Seasoned Citizen.

One of the most important factors in an older golfer's swing is the body turn. The older one gets, the harder it is to turn. Keeping the left heel down makes it all the harder. Don't raise the heel, just let it come up as it will want to do.

A straight left arm inhibits the turn. If a Seasoned Citizen has become heavy in the chest and stomach, there should be no effort made to keep a straight left arm at the top of the backswing. A player should try to swing longer, not shorter, as the years go by.

Another block to the swing is keeping the head down too long. I doubt I tell one student a month to keep his head down, and I almost never say it to an older player. Keeping the head down prevents a good follow-through because the golfer can't swing past hip-high with the head still down and not give up something good in the finish to do it.

Other than strong legs and plenty of stretching exercises, the first consideration for the older golfer is selecting the proper clubs.

You don't want to fiddle too much with a swing that has been useful to you for decades, but now is the time to add a 5- or 6-wood and especially a 7-wood to your bag. Seasoned Citizens get their loft from their clubs, not from their swing. Adding loft is a reliable substitute for youth and strength.

The older golfer must play with softer shafts. If you used "S" shafts when you were younger, switch to the "R" shafts. If you had been using "R" shafts, you may need to change to

"A" shafts. You are not hitting as hard as when you were young, and you can't get the most out of the stiffer shafts.

Men should use D-0 or lower swingweights. Women should use no more than C-6 or C-8.

Many Seasoned Citizens have problems with arthritis in their hands. Built-up grips are available to help you hold the club. Composition grips are best for arthritic golfers because they give a bit. Leather is not resilient enough.

I don't like to see the Seasoned player change to longer shafts in an effort to get more distance. A longer club causes a big change in the swing plane, from upright to flat. Flat swings require more turn, which is difficult for an older player.

If you can hit the ball solidly, you can get enough distance.

The Seasoned Citizen may want to try the ten-finger grip, which allows the hands to move faster.

One disadvantage older players may have is that they learned the game before the tremendous improvement in golf course maintenance, when it was necessary to hit down on the ball because the grass was sparse. Today's heavy, well-watered fairways make hitting down on the ball an out-of-date technique.

Many older golfers learned to play the ball far back in their stance for an iron shot. Modern fairways have done away with the need for that technique, also. Years ago we would play the ball off the right foot so we could hit down on it on the bare lies. Today the iron shots should be played no farther back than center.

A Seasoned Citizen should at regular intervals visit a professional who understands the problems of older golfers. You don't want a teacher who tries to rebuild a golf swing that you have been using for decades. You want a teacher who will help you get the best out of the swing you already have.

Perhaps most important of all, a Seasoned Citizen should devote at least 75 percent of practice time to the short game.

I harp on the significance of the short game to golfers of all ages. But this is an area where an older player who may have never broken 90 can expect to cut strokes. A retired person has the time to practice the short game. Short shots don't require strength or flexibility.

Don't plead that you are so old and your nerves so frayed that you can't putt. Every golf course has a few old geezers who can chip and putt the eyes out of the cup.

Certainly the older golfer can't hit the ball as far as the young, flat-bellied player. But once you reach the fringe of the green, you and the younger player become no worse than equals. And you can even have the advantage if you are faithful in practicing your short game.

Just as I suggest for children, the Seasoned Citizen will get the most out of chipping and putting practice by using just one golf ball to practice with instead of a whole basketful at a time.

Pitch or chip that one ball to the cup, and then go putt it until you make it, just as you would have to do if you were on the course playing a match. This sharpens your focus and improves your touch.

You have plenty of time. Make a game out of practice. You may be a Seasoned Citizen, but you know you're still a child at heart.

The Left Heel

THE LEFT HEEL is the subject of distinctly different schools of teaching.

Many modern teachers want their students to keep their left heel on the ground throughout the swing.

The old-school teachers like Percy Boomer and the great Scottish pros want the left heel to come up in the backswing and return to the ground at the start of the downswing.

I am of the old school, not because it produces a more classic swing—which it does—but because letting the left heel come up is the best way to get the job done.

The important thing is that you do not consciously lift the left heel. You keep the left heel on the ground, but you let it naturally come up as you make your back turn.

I think the reason Jack Nicklaus has such good control at the top is that he lets that left heel come up, releasing a full turn. He doesn't have to complete his backswing by letting loose of the club.

Ben Hogan never worried about his left heel. It either came up or it didn't, depending on the swing he was making.

Shelley Mayfield made the left-heel-on-the-ground swing popular in the middle '50s when he was a winner on the tour. Shelley, who became the head pro at Brook Hollow in Dallas, told me he didn't keep his left heel on the ground on purpose. It was just his natural, individual style.

Often when people imitate the swing of a top player, they will pick out a peculiarity to copy. The so-called flying elbow of Nicklaus or the open stance of Lee Trevino will be what they imitate.

Shelley told me he wished his left heel had let itself come up in his backswing, but it just wouldn't do it.

In my opinion, keeping the left heel flat on the ground throughout the swing will shorten the player's period of success.

Backspin

AN AVERAGE GOLFER was pestering Tommy Armour to teach him how to put backspin on his iron shots.

The obvious answer is that if you hit the ball solidly, the loft on the club will put backspin on it. But this was too simple. The average golfer was sure Tommy must know some secret that made a good middle-iron shot land on the green and dance backward.

Finally Tommy said, "Let me ask you something. When you hit an approach shot from 140 yards or so, are you usually past the pin, or are you usually short of it?"

"I'm nearly always short of the pin," the average golfer replied.

"Then what do you need with backspin?" Tommy said.

Heavy Clubs

EVERY GOLFER, FROM the young adult through Seasoned Citizens, should own a heavy practice club that weighs at least twenty-two ounces.

It hardly need be said that a heavy club is no good for children.

Swinging a weighted club, with your regular grip and stance, is the best exercise I know to build the golf muscles. Squeezing a tennis ball and similar exercises might be all right, but I'd be afraid the wrong muscles might get developed.

In golf you don't need muscles that lift weights. You want muscles that can pop a whip—or play golf.

Swing the weighted club the night before a round, not in the morning before you tee off. Save your strength for the golf course.

Don't swing it so hard you'll hurt yourself. If it is inconvenient to go outside, swing the weighted club indoors—in slow motion.

A slow-motion swing develops the golf muscles, implants the correct club positions in your golfing brain—and doesn't smash the chandelier.

Every time you swing that weighted club, slow or moderately fast, aim the clubhead at a fixed spot. Learn a good habit while you are building golf muscles.

*Harvey in plus-fours
(four inches below the knee).*

The Wrist Cock

I PREFER A SWING with a full, early wrist cock, but I don't like to use the words "wrist cock" because so many students become so entranced with getting their wrists cocked that they forget the rest of the swing.

One way to mess up students is to tell them to cock their wrists.

Women, especially, try to cock their wrists at the top of their backswing—and thus they overswing and lose snap.

When you swing back to waist high—the shaft parallel to the ground—the toe of the club must be pointed straight up to the sky.

If it is, your wrists will be cocked and you don't need to think about it. Go ahead and make your turn.

To get a clear picture in mind of how the wrists cock, double your left hand into a fist. This is an automatic wrist cock.

Make a golf swing with your left fist and you can immediately see what position the club is in when your wrists cock, then uncock, and cock again at the finish.

Look at your fist in a full-length mirror. The "wrist cock" will cease to be a source of confusion.

Hit a Full Approach

THE AVERAGE GOLFER seldom hits a middle-iron approach shot past the pin.

Some teachers recommend that the average golfer use one club stronger for his approach.

In other words, some say if you are 140 yards out and think the shot calls for a 7-iron, choose a 6-iron instead and hit it easier.

I don't care for this idea. I would much rather you take the 7-iron and hit it harder, with the thought in mind that you are going to get the ball all the way to the hole.

When you take a stronger club and try to hit it easy, your muscles will involuntarily tell you that you are using the wrong club, and you are likely to flinch and pull up on the shot.

If you want to hit the stronger club anyway, grip down an inch on the handle—and go ahead and hit it hard.

I like to see a golfer hit the bail hard if he doesn't swing so fiercely he loses his tempo and balance.

When Jimmy Thompson was the longest hitter on the tour, he enjoyed visiting me for guidance because he knew I was one teacher who would never tell him not to hit it so hard.

But always play within yourself.

The main reason so many approach shots come up short is that four out of five are hit off-center.

Bunker Play

PRACTICE YOUR BUNKER game to become more aggressive with it. You don't have to look at it as being in anticipation of your misses.

If you practice it and learn a few fundamentals, playing a ball out of a greenside bunker is not a difficult shot, even for the average golfer.

First, grip your sand wedge high on the handle as you would for a normal iron shot. This encourages you to take a full swing all the way to a high follow-through without quitting on the shot when the club strikes the sand.

Grip it tightly with the little finger and ring finger of your left hand so the club won't roll over and close in the sand.

Play the ball with the shaft pointing at your zipper and your hands slightly ahead. Take a square stance and open your clubface so that it points right of the target.

Then open your stance by moving your left foot back and taking your hips and shoulders with it, so that now your body is aimed left of the target but the clubface has come around to aim straight at it.

Shift a little more weight onto the left foot than on the right.

Now make a basically normal swing along the line established by your shoulders and body. Hit three or four inches behind the ball and clip the sand out from beneath it. The ball will come out and land on the green in a spray of sand.

Practice this shot for a few hours and you will see what I mean about becoming aggressive with it.

You won't need to worry again about merely escaping from the bunker somehow. You will be shooting at the pin.

The longer the shot, the less you hit behind the ball. The shorter the shot, the more sand you must take.

Don't Relax

YOU HEAR IT all the time on the range and on the course—relax, relax, relax.

I have even heard a golfer attempt to help a companion by saying, "Try real hard to relax."

If you try real hard to relax, you will become either very tense or else so limp you might fall over on the grass and go to drowsing.

Neither of those states is conducive to hitting a golf shot.

You do want to keep tension from creeping into your muscles, of course, and from allowing fear in your heart.

But I prefer to put it this way:

Be at ease.

If you feel at ease, you are relaxed—but ready.

The secret is the feeling of "controlled violence," as Jackie Burke, Jr., says.

Positive Thinking

WHEN I AM teaching, I never say never and I don't say don't, if I can help it.

I use the words "never" and "don't" in this book rather often, but that is because the reader has the leisure to reflect upon the point I am trying to get across.

But I would never say never and I don't say don't to a student on the range with club in hand and a need to learn while under the stress of being watched and mentally graded.

I try to put everything in positive, constructive terms. I go into this subject more deeply in my remarks on teaching, but the point I am trying to get across to the reader here is that when you are hitting a golf shot, a negative thought is pure poison.

I could have called this discussion "No Negative Thoughts"—but even that can be construed as a negative thought in the mind of a golfer.

Jack Burke, Sr., said it this way: "Give yourself the benefit of the doubt."

But even that statement has the dangerous word "doubt" in it.

I want you to believe with all your heart that the shot you are about to hit will be a good one. I want you to have total confidence.

This may sound ridiculous to the player who doesn't break 100. The difference is between confidence and optimism. Confidence is when you have hit this particular shot many times in the past with success, and you know you are capable of doing it again. Any 85-shooter has hit every shot in the bag with success many times. The ability is there. Optimism would be if you had never hit this shot successfully in your life, and are hoping this will be the first time.

The 100-shooter can be helped enormously by positive thinking, but he or she needs some groundwork of teaching upon which to base these positive thoughts before they can be distinguished as the feeling of confidence.

Indecision is a killer.

For example, when you pull that 5-iron out of the bag and register the target in your mind and address the ball, you must totally believe this is the right club for the shot. Put your best swing on it.

If it turns out the 5-iron was a club too much or too little but you hit it solidly, you won't be more than ten yards off.

However, if you can't make up your mind whether the shot calls for a 4-, a 5-, or a 6-iron, and you choose the 5 as a compromise, and then are still unsure when you take your stance, you might as well go sit down.

Many conflicting voices are chattering inside the mind of the average golfer. He or she is thinking of the latest swing "tips" heard on the veranda, and wondering if the club is going back too much inside and which "swing thought" might work at the moment, and probably worrying if the teenager remembered to put gas in the auto.

The golfer must learn to turn off all these voices.

A golf swing happens right now, not in the past or in the future.

Think positively and as my big brother Tom, the pro at Austin Muny for thirty years, used to say, "Rare back and hit it."

Psychology

A SPORTSWRITER WAS in town to interview Tom Kite at Austin Country Club. Sandra Palmer and I were standing around, sort of listening to the interview. The sportswriter turned to me and said, "Harvey, I understand you are practically a psychiatrist when it comes to golf."

"I don't know about that," I said. "I'm just a grown caddie still studying golf."

"You used psychology on me this morning," Tommy said.

"When was that?" I asked.

"When I asked you to help me with my putting," Tommy said. "You asked me if I had changed anything since the last time you saw me. I said, yes, I had started choking down on my putter."

"Tommy, don't use that word," I said. "You should never use the word 'choke' in connection with your golf game. Don't think of choking down on your putter—think of gripping down on it."

"That's what you told me this morning," he said. "That's psychology, isn't it?"

It always made me uncomfortable when Jimmy Demaret talked about his "choke stroke."

What Jimmy meant was he had in his repertoire a simple, reliable type of swing that he could call upon when he was under intense pressure. This swing wouldn't do anything fancy and wouldn't hit the ball as far as normal, but it was a repeating swing that would put his ball somewhere in the fairway or on the green

He should have called it a "no choke stroke."

Harvey practicing, 1938.

But I wouldn't have liked that either, because it still had the word "choke" in it, and also the word "no."

The golfing area of the brain is a fragile thing that is terribly susceptible to suggestion. Golfers are gullible.

I tell my players to go to dinner with good putters.

We have all played with people who would try to talk you into losing. They'll stand on the tee with an innocent expression and say, "Gee, look how tight that boundary marker is on the left. I sure hope I don't hit it over there." Or they might say, "That's an interesting change you've made in your backswing, Harvey." Maybe the best one I ever heard was when someone asked, "Do you breathe in or out on your backswing?"

We call these remarks "The Needle."

The Needle seldom bothers an experienced player. Instead, it's a giveaway that the person using The Needle is feeling insecure.

Playing golf you learn a form of meditation. For the four hours you are on the course, you learn to focus on the game and clean your mind of worrisome thoughts

Golf has probably kept more people sane than psychiatrists have.

Stay Behind the Ball

TRY TO SHOW me a champion who doesn't move his head during his golf swing. You can't do it. Sam Snead comes as close as anyone ever has, but he moves it too.

However, all these great players move their head slightly backward before and during impact—never forward.

Home-run hitters do the same thing. You'd see Hank Aaron blast one over the scoreboard, and people would say, "He really stayed behind that one."

A golfer also must stay behind the ball.

You couldn't kill a fly with a flyswatter if you lunged your head forward. To get power with a flyswatter you hold your head steady, or pull it back. Byron Nelson dropped his head back nearly a foot coming into the ball.

Before you can stay behind the ball, you must *get* behind it. I mean set up with your head behind the ball and keep your head behind the ball.

If you move your head forward during your downswing or through impact, you will hit a weak, ugly shot, probably a pulled slice.

A student told me about a round of golf he played with Lee Trevino.

On the second tee, a par three, the student hit what he thought was a pretty good shot, about thirty feet short of the pin.

Trevino tossed another ball onto the ground.

"Tee it up and hit it again—don't move your head forward this time," Trevino said.

"Lee, I've been trying all my life to stop moving my head forward," the student said. "How can I do it?"

Trevino said, "Read my lips. D-O-N'-T M-O-V-E Y-O-U-R H-E-A-D F-O-R-W-A-R-D. Every time you hit a ball today, I want you to think 'Lee is watching and saying read my lips.'"

The student was deeply impressed. He made another swing, this time without moving his head forward. With an authoritative crack, the ball took off in a slight draw, came down ten feet past the pin, and backed up.

"I have created a monster," Lee said.

The student finished the first nine one under par.

At the turn Lee put his clubs in the trunk of his car and

said, "I have to leave now, Frankenstein. Don't forget what I told you."

I asked the student what happened next.

"By the fourteenth hole my head was moving forward again," he admitted. "I shot my usual 41 on the back."

Maybe it was the word "don't" that made the suggestion not last long.

A positive way to put it is: *Stay behind the ball.*

Hitting From the Top

PROBABLY THE BIGGEST fault for all players has dozens of different names around the world. In England it is called Casting, which is a good description because the movement you make with your right arm and hand is similar to casting with a fly rod.

My friend Darrell Royal, an excellent golf player as well as the head coach of National Championship football teams at the University of Texas, has a colorful name for the fault I am talking about.

Darrell calls it OTTFIG. This translates to: "Over the Top, Forget It."

For this discussion, I will refer to the fault as Hitting From the Top.

Hitting From the Top is what happens when you reach the top of your backswing, and start back down to the ball by throwing your hands at it.

Many golfers play their whole lives Hitting From the Top. Some have managed to play well despite this flaw. Amateur Bud McKinney, a Texan who wore big flashy diamond rings, rang up an impressive record while Hitting From the Top. There are players on the professional tour who get outside the ball on their downswing, which is about the same thing as Hitting From the Top.

But just because some players are athletic enough to make this move and get away with it, doesn't make it any less disastrous for the average golfer.

No one has ever found an instant cure for this particular ailment.

Hard practice on sound fundamentals is a great help, of course, but that is not the answer a one-visit student wants to hear from an instructor.

Here are a number of things that cause Hitting From the Top:

- A grip that is too weak, especially the left hand.
- Misuse of the forearms, meaning the use of the wrists instead of the forearms at the beginning of the backswing and at impact.
- Aiming to the right.
- A stiff left leg at impact. I notice that the expert players who are least likely to Hit From the Top keep their knees slightly bent as they come through the ball. Telling a student to hit against a strong left side, which used to be common theory in teaching, tends to make the student start the downswing from outside the ball, straighten the left leg, and throw the club out and over the correct swing path.

  (To demonstrate this point, make a slow-motion swing keeping your knees slightly bent until after the ball is hit. The club will stay inside. Take another slow-motion swing and straighten your left leg about halfway down. Your upper body will throw itself out and over the ball.)

- The clubface too open at address.

But the question the instructor constantly confronts is, how to persuade the student to stop Hitting From the Top without becoming too technical or offering more advice than can be absorbed in one lesson.

I know five ways that have been successful for me.

The first and simplest is to make the student try to hit the ball on the toe of the club for a while. This is often a one-aspirin remedy for the sickness.

Another simple one is to place two balls on the ground about two inches apart and have the student hit the inside ball without touching the other.

A third and still simple method is for me to hold a shaft about a foot off the ground in front of the student and have him swing beneath it.

The fourth cure, the strongest and most basic, is to make the student learn to hook the ball. Strengthen the grip, rolling both hands to the right in exaggerated fashion. Tell the student to go ahead and hook the ball clear off the practice range. I don't care how much of a big wild hook, just as long as it is a hook.

I tell the student to rotate the left forearm to the right going back. Sometimes I have the student think of rotating the entire left arm. This fans the clubhead open on the backswing. Then bring the club down rotating the left arm and hand (the right hand automatically becomes involved) to the left and close the clubface hard at impact.

This process produces some of the most screaming fishhook-looking shots you ever saw.

But to hit these fishhooks, the student has to come into the ball from the inside.

Once a student learns to create hooks at will, he has usually stopped Hitting From the Top. The problem now becomes curing the hook. But this is relatively easy.

The fifth method is a slow-motion drill, and it's such an important drill that I want to hold it apart and explain it in a piece of its own.

I was demonstrating these methods at a PGA teaching seminar, using a waitress who had never played golf before as the student.

When we came to the fourth way, I was explaining to the pros in the crowd how this can cure the slice, and the waitress stopped me.

"Mr. Penick," she cried, "I don't want to be a hooker!"

The Slow-Motion Drill

THE SLOW-MOTION DRILL is a drill you can do at home, and it takes much patience and many repetitions, but the time you spend at it will pay off on the golf course.

Mickey Wright practiced this drill often. As an all-purpose drill that is good for whatever ails your golf swing, this is probably the best. You can do it indoors, so you can do it in bad weather or at night.

When I say slow motion, I mean *really slow, slow motion.* If you think you are doing it in slow motion, do it even slower.

Swing the club very slowly to the top of the backswing. *Always* keep your eye on the blade of grass or the pattern in the carpet that represents the golf ball; watching the clubhead go back is a terrible habit you can accidentally pick up in this drill and take to the course with you.

As you reach the top of the backswing, replace your left heel solidly on the ground and at the same time bring your right elbow in close to your body. Very, very slowly.

Bring the club down in extreme slow motion about one third of the way toward the ball. Then stop a moment and hold it and feel it.

Now start from your holding position and do it again—swing slowly to the top, plant the left heel, bring the right elbow close to the body, and stop about one third of the way toward the ball.

Do this four times in a row. Don't get impatient and speed up. Very slowly is the key.

After four repetitions, go ahead and make the full swing at last—still in very slow motion—into a high finish with the elbows out front and your head coming up slowly as if to watch a good shot. Hold the pose. Feel it.

Now do the whole thing again and again and again.

What is happening is that your golfing brain and your muscles are learning to start your downswing by planting your weight and moving your lower body to the left, and you are coming to the ball from inside with your hands quiet, trailing and still cocked, not leading and spending energy.

Your golfing brain and your muscles learn just as well from repeating the swing in slow motion as from whapping away on the range. In fact, it can be higher quality learning because no mistakes are being made in the slow-motion swing.

Ball Position

POSITION OF THE BALL is second in importance only to the grip.

Mistakes in grip and ball position are mistakes made before the swing that may ruin any grand plans you have for the shot.

Many instructors teach that the ball should be played off the left heel for all shots.

I don't agree with this. Good players can do it nowadays off good lies. But if you play the ball off your left heel with a 9-iron, you are going to have to have a terribly fast hip shift to meet the club with the ball on the downblow.

The driver and a teed-up 3-wood are the only clubs you want to play off your left heel. This is because you want to hit the ball slightly on the upswing or at the lowest point of the swing with these clubs.

With the rest of the clubs you move back a fraction of an inch at a time until you reach dead center, which is where the 9-iron belongs.

If you have any doubt where to position the ball for any iron, take a couple of practice swings and note where the clubface brushes the ground.

Another way is to put your iron down on the grass with a square face, and you will see where the manufacturer designed the club to be played.

Swing the Bucket

To START A GOLF swing you need a forward press of some sort that sets off the action.

My favorite image of what I want the forward press to feel like is to imagine you are in your stance holding a bucket of water with your hands on either side of the bucket.

If you're going to swing this bucket back like a golf backswing, you just naturally won't do it from a dead stop. Your hands and hips and shoulders and legs will rock forward a tiny bit to provide the reaction that gives momentum to the backswing. This starts the turn and the shift of the weight to the right foot that you would need to swing a bucket of water.

Your hands will follow your turn into the backswing as the bucket goes up. Your left heel will rise.

If you are gripping the bucket tightly, you will turn fast. If your grip is light, your turn will be slow and free.

To bring the bucket back down, you wouldn't throw it with your hands. You would shift your weight onto your left foot and turn your left hip, and you would naturally stay behind the bucket as you swing it down and through.

You can picture the release of power as the bucket reaches the forward swing and the water flies out.

A teacher I respect, Chuck Cook, suggests further in the swing-the-bucket image that if you tell your muscles to spill water to the left at the finish, you will hit a hook or draw, and if you spill it to the right, you will hit a fade.

The swing-the-bucket image works. It is especially easy to use to start a forward press.

The Penicks' first home in Austin.

Remember, don't overdo it. Just take a sip of medicine, not a great gulp.

The Weed Cutter

———

OF ALL THE THOUSANDS of swing-training aids and gimmicks I have seen, the best is one you can buy at the hardware store if you don't already have it in your garage or toolshed.

It is the common weed cutter.

Many years ago Victor East, the genius behind Spalding clubs, sent six weed cutters to me and six to Wild Bill Mehlhorn, who was teaching at a club in Florida.

A few weeks later Mehlhorn sent his weed cutters back to Victor with a note that said, "These things are ruining my business. Students who use them don't need me anymore."

The motion you make lopping off dandelions with your weed cutter is the perfect action of swinging a golf club through the hitting area.

Furthermore, the weed cutter is heavy and builds golf muscles.

While you are swinging the weed cutter, pretend you are being paid by the hour, not by the job.

In other words, take your time.

Placing Your Feet

MOST PLAYERS, INCLUDING many experts, fail to grasp what a big difference in the length of the swing is caused by the positions of the feet.

Try this and see for yourself. Take a normal stance and turn back to the top of your backswing with your shaft pointing at the target. Look in the mirror. Now set up again. This time turn your left foot out and down the line enough to cut out a good slice of pie. Make your backswing as before. Look in the mirror again. What do you see? Your backswing is several inches shorter.

Set up again with your left foot in a natural position, but bring your right foot square to the line or even point it a bit toward the target. Make your backswing. See? Again your backswing is several inches shorter.

Many players set up with their left foot splayed way out and their right foot square or turned in—a combination guaranteed to shorten the backswing dramatically.

An average player will adopt this stance because he thinks this is what he sees the pros do. Then he will wonder, where did my turn go?

These foot positions have no real effect on where you are aiming, but they are very important in the length of your swing.

The Turn

THE TURN AWAY from the ball and back through it again is a simple movement that has been made to seem complicated by differing teaching theories and personal idiosyncrasies.

As Horton Smith would say, the turn is just like that song children used to sing, "The ankle bone connected to the knee bone, the knee bone connected to the hip bone, the hip bone connected to the back bone, the back bone connected to the shoulder bone . . . Now hear the word of the Lord."

Do it this way and keep it simple:

Stand erect with your knees slightly flexed and your eyes on the ball. Think of your swing-the-bucket image to start your forward press. Turn your body to the right with your weight shifting to your right foot, and let your left heel gently come up about an inch. It's like turning to say howdy to someone on your right. Your arms keep swinging until your shaft is behind you and points to the target.

Now let your weight shift back to your left foot at the same time your right elbow starts back toward your side, and continue turning as if to say howdy to someone on your left.

You will read and hear many complex instructions about the turn—coiling the torso and shoulders against the tension of the hips, for example—but not from me.

I have seen a lot of players who are so concerned with their hip turn they forget that swinging the golf club is the main point. Just remember the turn is a natural movement of the body, and your bones are connected from the ground up.

Instant Humility

———

In our hotel room I was nervously going over my notes for the lecture I was to present in a few hours to a large audience of my peers at a PGA convention.

I was starting to feel a little impressed with myself. Here I was, a humble growing caddie, about to give a speech on how to teach golf to a room crowded with the best golf teachers in the world.

"Just consider it, Helen," I said. "Of all the great teachers, they have chosen me to make this talk. How many great teachers do you suppose will be there?"

My lovely wife looked up from the book she was reading.

"I don't know how many great teachers will be there, Harvey," she said. "But it's probably one less than you think."

Maxims

———

In 1943 Jack Burke, Sr., compiled a list of golf maxims that grew out of discussions with players and teachers, one of whom was me.

1. The wrists play very little part in golf. The crossing of the forearms puts the punch in the golf shot.
2. The face of the club going off the line produces more poor shots than anything I know of.
3. If the club goes back properly there isn't much chance of a bad shot. (*I can't go along with this. For one thing, Jack taught an inside-out swing. I like a swing that is inside-square-inside. What Jack calls taking the club back properly means different things to different people. And many mistakes are made starting down from the top of the backswing. But I agree that if you start the club back properly, you are way ahead. What is proper for you is just to start the club back with your turn.*)
4. Split the ball in half in your mind and play the inside half; the outer half shouldn't be entertained. (*This is too much to think about. Just hit it.*)
5. Learn to pick the ball clean—don't hoe it.
6. Picture a shot going perfectly to the line.
7. If the hands are joined together as one unit, you would be surprised the amount of relaxation attained.
8. Knock the peg from under the ball. This helps to get the club straight through. (I use this image constantly in my teaching—just clip off the tee with your swing.)
9. Let the ball get in the way of the swing instead of making the ball the object.
10. Don't try to pick the ball up—the club is built for that purpose.
11. Hitting behind the ball is caused by the weight being on the back foot. If the weight is forward it is impossible to hit behind the ball.

12. The reason for not going forward is tenseness—keep the hands together, then the move forward is easy.

13. Picture the shot as you would *like* to see it.

14. Keep your feet moving to the line of flight. Don't let them freeze to the ground.

15. The shank shot is caused by the club being on the outside of the ball. The heart stops but the mouth doesn't. Put two balls together two inches apart; if you can miss the outside ball, the shank shot is cured. (*I don't agree with the cause and have more to say about this in my remarks on the shank.*)

16. Have a little power left—don't put it all in the swing. You may need it before the game is over.

17. Let the club go where you expect the ball to.

18. Finishing the swing is very important. Without a good finish, to keep the ball straight is luck.

19. Get a system of some kind in playing. Any kind of a system beats trusting to luck.

20. Topping the ball is caused by closing the face of the club toward the body. (*I think more often topping the ball is caused by stiffening the knees.*)

21. Slicing is caused by the hands leading the head of the club. Tenseness plays a major part. The face of the club is not flush at impact.

22. Anyone slicing the ball has reached the top of his game. The harder he hits it, the more it will slice.

23. A ball lying badly, better try to pick it in preference to hoeing it out.

24. Be honest with yourself. What you would find out in six months of practice, your pro can tell you in five minutes.

25. Hit the ball, then the ground—that will assure you of getting down to the ball.

26. Let the right hip take the club back and the left hip bring the club forward.
27. Try holding your right shoulder back as long as possible to give your left side a chance to get through.
28. Hold the head of the club off the ground if you are inclined to be tense.
29. Let the hands start slightly before the head of the club on the backswing.

The Mythical Perfect Swing

HERE IS HOW to make the Mythical Perfect Swing that all golfers are always pursuing:

Stand a few paces behind the ball and look down the line toward the target.

Walk to the ball from behind, get a good grip, pass the club back of the ball square to the target, then adjust your stance to fit.

Have a slight waggle and then set the club back of the ball again and make a forward press similar to what you would do swinging a bucket of water.

In the first move back as the club gets parallel to the ground, the toe of the club points directly up, and the left heel starts off the ground.

Let the club come on up, keeping your elbows in front of your body, to the top of your backswing, where the club-head will be pointing almost to the ground.

Return your left heel to the ground and simultaneously

let your right elbow move back to your side as it comes down.

Weight has started shifting to your left side. Your forearms cross over as they swing. Your head stays behind the ball, perhaps even moving slightly more behind it.

Finish with your forearms in front of you. A good finish shows what has gone before it. Let your head come up to look at the good shot.

On your follow-through, the right foot merely helps to hold your balance.

If you have lost your balance during this Mythical Perfect Swing, it is probably because your grip is too weak or too tight or both.

Practice this at home in slow motion without a ball.

Be sure you don't watch the clubhead go back. Swing the clubhead at a spot every time.

Force yourself to approach the ball from behind before every swing, even on the carpet.

Make ten to twenty Mythical Perfect Swings each night, teaching your muscles what your brain wants.

Using a weighted club during this exercise can be even more beneficial.

The Magic Move

If there is any such thing as a Magic Move in the golf swing, to me it is an action that I stress over and over on the practice tee and in this book.

You have heard it from me many times by now, but I will say it again—*to start your downswing, let your weight shift to your left foot while bringing your right elbow back down to your body.*

This is one move, not two.

Practice this move again and again. You don't need a golf club to do it. Practice until you get the feeling and rhythm of it, and then keep on practicing. Be sure your eyes are trained on the spot where the ball would be. Your head will stay well back.

I've read books and magazines that offered the "secret" of The Move. The secret takes different forms for different players. For Ben Hogan the move is *pronating*. For Byron Nelson the move is *a lateral shift and not pronating*.

There really is no one Magic Move.

But when you learn the *left foot–right elbow* move I have described above, you will hit the ball as if it is magic.

How to Practice the Full Swing

———

CHOOSE A 7-IRON or a 6-iron, whichever one you feel the most confidence in, and use it for 80 percent of all your full-swing practice.

The reason for this is I want you to develop faith in your golf swing.

The best way to learn to trust your swing is by practicing your swing with a club you trust.

A high handicapper who learns to hit a good 7-iron can build his or her game around that shot. Even if you have to hit the ball twice on a par four to come within range of your 7-iron, it's a great help to know for sure that your 7-iron shot will land on the green. This will give you a putt at par

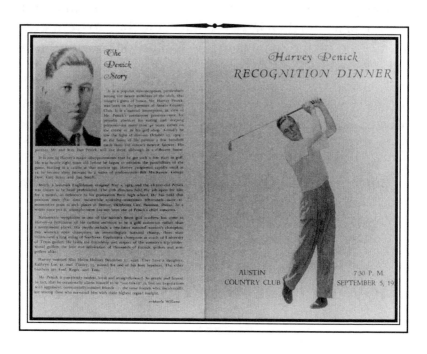

Program for the Harvey Penick Recognition Dinner, 1953.

even though the first two shots might have been poor efforts.

A full 7-iron swing is just about as long as a driver swing. It's the difference in length and the lie of the clubs that makes the driver swing look longer at the top of the backswing.

The main difference in swinging a 7-iron and a driver is that you want to hit your driver slightly on the upswing, or at the lowest point of the swing, and this is a function of ball position.

Some teachers have their students practice with a 3-iron on the theory that if the student can learn to hit a 3-iron, the rest of the clubs will seem easy.

This is certainly true, but it seems backward to me. It is much easier to learn to hit a good 7-iron, and that in turn will make the 3-iron easier to hit if you just use your good 7-iron swing on it.

Remember that because the number on the iron is lower does not mean you should swing the club harder.

Certainly you must practice a little with every club. But don't devote too much time to the driver. The driver is the most difficult club to hit, which is why they let you put the ball on a peg. The idea of practice is to improve—or at least to hold your own—and the surest way to do this is by practicing with a club that gives you good results.

I hate to see a high handicapper practicing the driver. It gets very ugly. The golfer becomes frustrated, and the swing gets worse and worse. Most high handicappers or once-a-week players should lock the driver in a closet and practice and play with a 3-wood.

If the average golfer hits the 3-wood off the tee, the shots will on the whole be more successful. What you will miss is maybe that one good driver shot in a round, and it's not worth it.

Warming Up in a Hurry

IF YOU ARRIVE at the course with just a few minutes to warm up before a round, use that time to hit chip shots.

The chip shot, being a short version of the full swing, tells your muscles and your golfing brain to get ready to play.

Most average golfers with only a few minutes to warm up will rush to the range and try to hit balls fast. This may loosen up the grease, but it also can ruin your tempo for the day and perhaps implant negative thoughts.

Some average golfers think they are wiser because they rush to the putting green instead, and try to hit as many putts as possible before being called to the tee. This is just as bad as rushing on the range. You'll probably miss a lot of those putts you're in such a hurry to hit, and by the time you tee off you will be doubting your putting ability.

To warm up in a hurry and arouse your sense of feel or touch, use the time you have to stroke a few careful chip shots.

This will put your mind on the business at hand—which is to play golf. If your mind is still back at the office when you go to the first tee, you are in for a rough day.

Chipping

THE FIRST AND foremost fundamental to learn about chipping is this: Keep your hands ahead of or even with the clubhead on the follow-through. All the way through.

Grip your club down close to the steel. Flex your knees so you can get down to it. Keep the club near to you, instead of reaching out for the ball. Move your weight a little more to your left foot.

Loosen your elbows. Remember that you are hitting the ball with your hands, not with your elbows.

Make your backswing and your follow-through approximately the same length, as in the putting stroke.

Use the straightest-faced club that will carry the ball onto the green the soonest and start it rolling toward the cup.

Off a downhill lie or a tight lie or into the wind or with a fast green, always choose to chip the ball rather than pitch it.

Under pressure around the green, always go to the straightest blade that will do the job. It may require a 3-iron to get the roll you need.

High handicappers should use their putters from off the green whenever it looks feasible. They'll generally get closer to the hole this way.

Putting

JUST AS IN chipping, the first and foremost fundamental to learn about the putting stroke is: Keep the hands even with or ahead of the head of the putter on the follow-through.

There are many great putters—like Billy Casper and Chi Chi Rodriguez—who use a wristy stroke and pop the ball as the clubhead passes their hands.

If I see a student using that sort of stroke and making a lot of putts, I won't try to change it. Putting is an individual matter. Bobby Locke hooked his putts. I would never try to teach a student to putt that way, but I sure wouldn't try to make Bobby Locke stop it.

The way I teach you to putt is by using a simple system.

Read your line from behind the ball. Walk to the ball from behind and take your stance with your hands slightly ahead of the ball or straight up. Glance at the hole and glance at your putter blade to make sure it is square to your line.

Now take one, two, or three practice strokes, concentrating on each one as if you are trying to make the putt, judging the distance. I like to see the stroke start with a small forward press, using the swing-the-bucket image.

Then put your putter blade down behind the ball, keep your head and eyes still, and imitate your last practice stroke.

One great value to this system is that it puts your mind on the stroke and not on the importance of the putt. Never—I repeat, never—allow yourself to think about what is riding on the putt, whether it's a major championship or just a fifty-cent wager. Hit the putt as you have hit ten thousand putts in the past. Concentrate on imitating your final practice stroke, not on what will happen if you either miss it or make it.

When practicing putting, always choose a level place on the green, or perhaps one that is slightly uphill.

I hate the old saying "never up, never in."

It's true that a ball that never reaches the cup never goes in, but neither does a ball that goes past it.

I like a putt to die at the hole. A putt that dies at the hole will sometimes topple in, whereas a putt that is struck too hard will hit the hole and spin away. Just as many putts are missed behind the hole as short of it.

The cup is only one inch wide for a putt that is struck too hard. The cup is four inches wide for a ball that dies at the hole.

Furthermore, it is much easier to sink a putt when you've left it a foot short than when you've gone three feet past, especially if it is uphill from the cup.

The main reason a putt is left short is not that you hit the putt too softly, it's that you didn't hit it squarely on the sweet spot.

I like to see a putt slip into the hole like a mouse.

One thing all great putters have in common, regardless of their style, is that the putting stroke is approximately the same length back and through.

Try to keep the putter low to the ground, but don't give up a good stroke to do it artificially.

With short putts, concentrate on the line.

With long putts, concentrate on the distance.

I prefer a putting stroke that uses the arms and wrists. But on a very long putt, you will need to use your shoulders and take a longer backswing and follow-through.

Play the ball off the left heel. Place your feet square to the line.

If you are taking the putter too much outside the line, your weight could be on your toes and your eyes might not be over the ball.

There are two reliable ways to be sure your eyes are over the ball. Either hold a ball at eye level and then drop it and see where it lands, or else hold your putter shaft straight down from eye level to the ball.

To take your grip, put your left hand on the putter the way the manufacturer designed the grip to be held. Most great putters have their right hand under a little and keep the blade square because they offset it by weakening the left hand.

Once you adopt a good system for putting, the rest of it is mental. Stay with your system.

I was at the Masters watching them play, and I noticed Jacky Cupit on the practice green. I watched him awhile and finally couldn't stand it. I walked over and said, "Jacky, would you mind if I make a suggestion?"

He said, "Why do you think I've been staying close to the rope all this time?"

He had been hitting a pulled hook with his putter. Trying to correct it, he had yanked his hands way up high. I said, "Son, let's try holding that putter the way the man who made the grip intended for you to hold it. Just make your hands fit it."

Jacky went out and shot a 67, low round of the day until Ben Hogan came in with a 66. Jacky showed me his scorecard with a happy grin and said, "Harvey, we did it!" I hadn't really done anything except give him a positive thought.

I hear people talk about hitting putts with overspin. I say this is nearly impossible. It's like in shooting pool; to put overspin on a pool ball, you have to hit it with the cue tip on the top seven tenths of the ball. You don't want to try to hit a putt like that.

A good putt dies out straight. A bad putt slithers away.

Be decisive on the putting green. Decide what you want to do on a putt and then do it with confidence, even if it should prove to be wrong.

You should make it a habit to carry your putter in your left hand. Or in both hands, if you wish. But never carry it in your right hand alone.

Your left hand and arm are an extension of the putter shaft. That is the feeling you want to have.

I see pros on the tour place the putter behind the ball with their right hand. Then when they put their left hand on the club, they have automatically changed their aim.

Put your putter behind the ball with your left hand, or with both hands.

Think positively.

The reason I am so hipped on putting is two of my best friends were the best putters of their time—Horton Smith and Ben Crenshaw.

Horton Smith used a practice putting drill that I recommend. Stroke a few putts using only your right hand. When you get the feeling for it, allow your left hand to join in gently. But I like both hands to work together.

A good drill for developing touch is to putt a ball 30 feet. Then putt the next one 29 feet. Then 28 feet, and so on.

Play games on the putting green. The more time you spend there, the better golf scores you will turn in.

The Dreaded Four-Footer

A WOMAN AT church remarked to me, "Harvey, that game you play doesn't make sense. You hit a ball 250 yards off the tee and it counts one stroke, the same as for a three- or four-foot putt."

Not even the most expert of golfers would argue the point with her. At his home club, Shady Oaks in Fort Worth, Ben Hogan likes to play fairways and greens and closest to the pin, leaving out putting entirely.

Orville Moody said the four-foot putt almost ran him off the tour. "I just can't get over the fact that I can hit two great shots covering maybe 440 yards, and be four feet from the cup, and if I miss that little-bitty putt it counts as much as the two great shots," he said.

This was before Orville got his extra-long putter and started winning big money on the Senior Tour. (Being old-fashioned, I don't like the extra-long putters. They look funny to me. I think there should be a rule in golf that the two hands must touch each other.)

One of the 85-shooters at my club told me, "Harvey, I'd rather face a 175-yard carry across a lake than a four-foot putt."

Teaching seminars I would often start by saying, "Getting up in front of you teaching professionals makes me more nervous than anything except a three-foot downhill putt that breaks to the left on a slick green."

(Upon reading that statement, many of you are probably saying, "Harvey got it backward. Everybody knows a down-hill putt that breaks to the right is the hardest putt for a right-hander.")

Just let me say that in many years of conducting seminars for up to 250 pros in a class, not a one of them ever argued with me about the left-breaking downhill putt causing their nerves to get jumpy.

The fact is that both the left- and right-breakers are very difficult. The reason I say the left-breaker is hardest is that you aim to the right of the hole and your stroke tends to come from the inside, hooking the ball through the break.)

Let's think a moment about these dreaded short putts and see if we can remove some of the fear.

An average golfer misses short putts because of fear or a lack of concentration. Instead of thinking about stroking the putt into the hole, he or she is thinking about any number of things—including the other players who are standing on the green watching for the result.

The average player usually doesn't work as hard lining up a three- or four-footer as lining up a ten-footer that might be an easier putt.

Another major mistake I see in average golfers is that they try to guide the short putt into the hole. They try to use their stroke to steer the ball through the break.

The right way to do it is to approach the short putt from behind and line it up. If you decide it breaks two inches left of the cup then that's where you want to stroke it—not jerk it toward the hole.

Use the system. Make one, two, or three practice strokes, concentrating on the line, washing bad thoughts out of your mind. Then imitate your last practice stroke. Don't look up and peek at it. Just stroke it on the line. This routine helps to keep your thoughts from being distracted.

Negative thoughts and carelessness cause more missed short putts than any other factor.

If it's a downhill putt that breaks to the left, an aspirin is to stroke the ball on the toe of the putter. This removes some or all of the break.

When I tell students this, they always ask, "Does that mean I should hit the putt on the heel if it breaks the other way?"

My answer is no. Never hit it on the heel.

A three- or four-footer that is straight will always go in if you stroke the ball in the sweet spot on the putter face, provided you are aimed at the center of the cup.

Don't worry about anything but the line. You'll hit the ball hard enough.

Be careful in lining up the short ones. Use the system and believe in what you're doing.

The greatest players in the world miss short putts, but not very often. There's no reason you should miss them, either.

The Shank Shot

———

A SHANK SHOT is so ugly that I hate to write the word.

Let's call it a Lateral Shot instead.

I had a student, a good player, who started hitting these Lateral Shots all of a sudden. He called me to the range and showed me.

Knowing he was a good player and thinking he would work his own way out of it, I said, "I'll bet you can't do that twelve times in a row."

So he stood there and did it twelve times in a row.

"Now what?" he said.

"Go home and come back tomorrow," I said.

Most people think this shot is caused by hitting the ball with a closed blade at impact, but this is improbable. Usually the shot is caused by blocking off a pull, or what you think is going to be a pull.

The ball may be too far forward. Beginners may be standing too close to it. Experienced players may be standing too far back.

Many times it is caused by the player trying to hold his or

her head down too much. This drops the head way down and extends the arc of the club, resulting in a bent left arm at impact.

Or it can be caused by poor eyesight. Any pilot will tell you eyesight will change a bit from day to day.

Cures for the Lateral Shot:

Try conscientiously to hit every iron shot on the toe of the club until you stop shanking.

Never aim to the left. You would do well to think you are aimed to the right.

Feel like the toe of the club is rolling over.

Place a pasteboard box or a tee about one inch outside of the ball lined up at the target. Hit the ball without hitting the box or the tee.

It is almost impossible to hit a Lateral Shot if the blade is closed. Try it sometime. Close the blade and make your best swing and follow through. Keep it closed throughout the swing. The ball may go to the left—but I don't think you can hit it laterally.

Why I Decided to Become a Teacher

SAM SNEAD.

I thought I was a pretty fair player and had nagging aspirations to join the tour until a Houston Open in the middle 1930s.

I was practicing putting and one of the fellows said, "Harvey, have you seen this kid Snead hit the ball? He's about to tee off now."

I walked over to the tee and saw the new kid from West Virginia hit his drive. I not only saw it, I heard it.

It sounded like a rifle and the ball flew like a bullet.

I knew right that moment that my future was not as a tour player.

The Stance

FACE THE BALL plain, as if you are about to shake hands with someone on the other side of it. There's no need to get your body twisted into some kind of funny shape. If you were going to shake hands with someone, you wouldn't bend sideways or slump sharply forward like so many beginners do.

If you are slew-footed by nature, it's better to point your toes out the way you walk. If you are pigeon-toed, you'll want your feet more square.

The Hogan foot position is preferred by many good players. This has the right foot square to the line and the left foot turned toward the target a few inches. The advantage of this is that the square right foot helps shorten a too-long backswing, and the slanted left foot helps to make a full weight shift and follow-through.

The average golfer may want the right foot toed out slightly to allow for more turn.

If you want to close your stance, pull your right foot back a few inches from the line. But be sure you turn your hips and shoulders to fit it. So many average golfers think if they just pull back the right foot, they have closed their stance. In fact, if they pull back the right foot but leave the hips and shoulders square, they haven't made any change at all.

To open your stance, pull your left foot back a few inches from the line and let your hips and shoulders go with it.

When you stand to the ball, just flex the knees a little, as if you are making the first move toward sitting down. When I tell students to flex the knees, so often they start jiggling up and down, which looks very amateurish.

I am careful about using this "sitting-down" thought, because the next time I see the student he or she may have swallowed the whole bottle of medicine and really be in a posture that looks like sitting in a chair.

Be comfortable and at ease, not straining anything.

Wesley Ellis, Jr., who played for me in college before he went on the tour, had the most natural-looking stance I ever saw. Wesley just walked up to the ball in his normal stride, stopped, and hit it. He kept the ball in play more than anyone I know of.

Wesley used to have a dog that would follow him faithfully on rounds of golf at Brackenridge Park. The dog would sit quietly, never bothering anyone. What a fine companion.

A Very Bad Habit

WATCHING THE CLUBHEAD go back as you start your swing will probably ruin any chance you have of hitting a good shot.

Anything you do wrong taking the clubhead back is not as bad as watching it.

It is amazing how many golfers get into this habit.

The First-Time Student

BEFORE I TAKE a student onto the range, I like to go into the clubhouse for a cup of coffee and a chat.

Usually students are nervous. I want to put them at ease. I want to gain their confidence. I ask about their game, how often they play or practice, what their goals are.

I tell them, "Any mistakes that are made out there today are mine, not yours."

When I hear one of my students griping about how his clubs are no good, I like to say, "Hey, your swings are my fault first of all, your fault second, and the club maybe third."

I'll ask the new student if he or she would rather hit woods or irons, are there any aches or pains, how is life going. I want to understand my students and put them at ease with me.

This takes about twenty minutes, and it gets us off on the right foot.

Kids and Carts

IN MY OPINION, no young player can develop his or her game to its highest potential if he or she rides around the course in a golf cart.

If they are old enough to swing a club, they should be walking, strengthening their legs, learning to feel the rhythm of the game that simply cannot be learned in a golf cart.

It's all right for youngsters to ride on a cart with Dad or Mom and have fun. But four youngsters driving around the course in two carts is a sad sight.

Walter Hagen said to stop and smell the flowers while you're on the course. This sensitivity is a powerfully alluring and educational part of golf. You're much less likely to realize it if you grow up riding in a cart.

A Story by Helen

WHEN WE GOT married sixty years ago, Harvey already had a big reputation in golf. He became head pro at Austin Country Club at eighteen and golf coach at Texas at twenty-six. So I was always known as Mrs. Harvey Penick. Only our friends knew me as Helen.

People would say, "She's Mrs. Harvey Penick. She's bound to know how to play golf." I loved the game, but I was an 18-handicapper. I finally started using my maiden name—Helen Holmes—when I would enter a tournament.

The last time I played with Harvey was in a Scotch Foursome at the old Austin Country Club on Riverside Drive. We were matched against Martha and Peck Westmoreland from Lockhart.

Before we teed off, Harvey told me, "Helen, Peck is hitting the ball so bad. It's his grip. Would you mind riding in the cart with Martha while I see if I can help Peck?"

Helen Penick, 1949.

After six holes, Peck was playing very well. Harvey came to me and said, "Helen, Martha is having a terrible time with her putting stroke. Would you ride with Peck for a while, and I'll try to help Martha."

Martha took two putts on the seventh and one-putted the eighth and ninth.

On the tenth tee I said, "Harvey, you helped Martha and Peck. Now tell me what I am doing wrong."

Harvey said, "I don't know. I haven't been looking."

So I quit playing with him.

He used to give me a fifteen-minute lesson and then go hide.

But maybe that's one reason we've stayed married so long.

Learning

I LEARN TEACHING from teachers.

I learn golf from golfers.

I learn winning from coaches.

There are many good teachers of golf who teach quite differently from each other. I prefer listening to one who teaches differently than I do. I might learn from him. I already know my own way.

The piano master Horowitz told his students, "Never be afraid to dare. Never be afraid to play without asking advice. I'm not going to teach you, but to guide you."

I read that quote to Tinsley, and he said, "Why, that sounds just like you."

I'll always remember what my cousin, Dr. D. A. Penick,

said when he turned over the reins as University of Texas tennis coach to Wilmer Allison:

"Wilmer, I know you'll make better players of your students in four years. But will they be better people? That's the important thing."

Ben Hogan

I WAS PLAYING in a charity match in Austin with Ben Hogan, and I heard him ask his caddie, "Which way is due west?"

It was a surprise to hear Hogan ask a caddie a question. Ben thought he knew his own game better than a caddie ever could. Ben judged his own distances and pulled his own clubs.

I wondered all day why Ben had asked that question. After the round, I brought it up.

"All other things being equal, greens break to the west," Ben said.

He is right, of course. There are many reasons why, I later found out, but unless the architect has tricked up the green to fool you, your putt will break to the west.

As a young man, Ben had a very bad pull hook. He worked it out himself, getting a good grip with his right hand well on top, the V pointing to his chin.

Pronation is what he called his secret. In the hitting area, his left forearm, or possibly his entire left arm, uncoiled. This got him inside the ball and gave him a snap.

Ben practiced thousands of hours perfecting his swing. At first he felt his swing was too long. He changed his stance to shorten his swing a little by adopting what is now the famous Hogan Stance—the right foot square to the line and the left toe turned out a few inches. Each of these foot movements shortens the backswing.

I like a long swing if it is kept under control, and Ben certainly learned to do that.

Jimmy Demaret and Hogan became pals. Jimmy told me he called up Ben before the first Legends of Golf Senior Tournament and asked Hogan to be his partner.

Ben replied he wasn't playing often or well.

"Come on and let's have some old-time fun," Jimmy said.

Ben said, "No, I couldn't help you."

Jimmy said, "So what? You never did."

The Sexes

No PRETTY WOMAN can miss a single shot without a man giving her some poor advice.

A husband should never try to teach his wife to play golf or drive a car. A wife should never try to teach her husband to play bridge.

A Practice Rule

NEVER PRACTICE YOUR full swing when the wind is blowing at your back. If you're right-handed, this means the wind is left to right. The more you practice with the wind blowing left to right, the more you will be inclined to swing across the ball and hit from the top.

Ben Hogan was one of the first to realize this.

Ben would seek out a part of the course where the wind was blowing into his face, either right to left or head-on, and that's where he would practice.

If you practice into the wind, just use your regular swing. Don't try to hit it harder. And please be careful not to practice too many "punch" shots. There's no follow-through on a "punch" shot.

Hooking and Slicing

HOOKS DON'T HURT the average golfer. It's the pulled hook that does the damage. If the average golfer is hitting a shot that flies straight and hooks toward the end, don't worry about it.

If your ball starts immediately to the left, and then hooks, you need help from a pro.

The first place to look is your grip. Take the privilege of making the V's of one or both hands point at your chin.

When one cures a hook by putting the left hand too much on top of the club, it is only a matter of time before the swing gets out and over the ball.

In your swing, concentrate on clipping the tee or brushing the grass. This will take the club straight through.

Opening the face of your club a little at address is practically the same thing as weakening your grip.

The slicer has a much worse time of it than the hooker.

Many high handicappers hit a slice as such a regular thing that they allow for it when they take aim. If you allow for a slice, you are almost certainly going to get one. (Allowing for a hook is also conducive to hooking.)

The slicer should first hold the club lightly and look to the grip.

You have the privilege to make your V's of either or both hands point to your right shoulder.

Again, clip the tee or brush the grass to make your clubface go straight through. Make sure to hold the club lightly. Think of it as a fine musical instrument. You wouldn't try to play a clarinet by crushing it, would you? Hold it lightly all the way through the swing.

A sure cure for the slicer is to pretend you are on a baseball field at home plate. Take your stance to aim your body slightly to the right of second base, but aim your clubface straight at the base. Then hit the ball over the shortstop. Use a 7-iron at first, then a 3-wood.

Be careful the downswing is not from the outside. Come down the line on plane and hit a hard fly ball over the shortstop, using primarily the left forearm and possibly rotating the whole left arm. This is the best cure for slicing that I know.

Read this carefully and I'm sure you can hook the ball.

Long and Short

JACK BURKE, JR., and I were giving a clinic and somebody asked about shooting at the flag with a long iron.

"I shoot at the middle of the green on long irons," Jack said. "Sometimes the ball rolls up by the flag and makes me look good."

Anybody who can play golf very well can shoot at the flag from 150 yards if the greens are soft. When the course is dry, most players will try to hit the ball too far off the tee and will wind up where they can't play to the pin.

There's no reason why the average golfer should take more than three to get down from 150 yards. If you spend most of your full-swing practice on your 7-, 6-, or 5-iron—whichever is your 150-yard shot—you will develop the confidence to hit the middle of the green, and maybe it will roll close to the cup and make you look good.

Chip or Pitch?

ALWAYS CHIP THE BALL if:

1. The lie is poor.
2. The green is hard.
3. You have a downhill lie.
4. The wind has an influence on the shot.
5. You are under stress.

Probably you want to pitch the ball if:

1. The lie is good.
2. You have an uphill lie.
3. The green is very soft.
4. There is an obstacle in the way.

Ability must be considered. The expert player can play a delicate chip with a sand wedge that would be very risky for a high handicapper. These are general guidelines.

A common fault in pitching is for the player to pull up off the shot. This is because the clubhead gets ahead of the hands. To cure this, I will have a student practice hitting a low pitch, as if he wants to hit a shot that would go under a card table. This encourages the student to stay down with the ball and let the loft on the clubhead do the pitching.

Hitting a pitch shot with a sand wedge from any distance, use the full length of the club. Gripping down on a sand wedge is conducive to chili-dipping, which is dropping your head and bending your left arm at impact, causing you to hit behind the ball or else top it.

Never let the clubhead pass your hands on the follow-through of a chip or a short pitch.

There is an important wedge shot to learn for close lies and winter fairways when the grass is dormant. Play the ball off the right foot. Close the blade until it is square to the line and the bounce of the blade does not touch the ground. Adjust your stance forward to compensate for direction. Put slightly more weight on the left foot. Strike the ball and the ground at the same time on the downswing.

This will produce a lower ball with more backspin. It is not a trick shot. It's a shot that comes in handy.

I taught this shot to one of my favorite students, former state senior champion Bill Penn.

He came in and complained, "Harvey, I want a shot that works 100 percent of the time. This one only works three out of four times for me. I two-putted once."

Preparing for a Big Match

BE YOURSELF. Do as you usually do. If you ordinarily have a couple of drinks in the evening, do it. If you have been going to bed at 11 P.M., do not crawl between the sheets two hours earlier than normal. Eat the same food you usually eat, and at the same hour.

You must understand that it is your mind that will have the most to do with how you play in the big match.

That's why you should avoid new or different things that will distract your mind from your normal routine.

Put the results of the big match out of your thoughts. The results are in the future. You want to stay in the present.

At the course before the big match, warm up as usual. If you ordinarily put on your shoes, hit half a dozen balls and go to the tee, keep it the same. Hitting a whole bag of balls will only hurt you, unless you always warm up with a whole bag.

This is no time to make a change in your swing or your grip. You must "dance with what brung you."

When you go to the first tee, don't even consider the eventual result of the round. Consider the shot at hand. Sandra Haynie, an LPGA Hall of Famer who grew up in Austin and Fort Worth, would not watch her opponents hit their shots. I don't necessarily recommend this for everyone, but it may help you stay concentrated on your own shot.

Try and play each shot to the best of your ability, one shot at a time—and *take dead aim!*

Playing in the Wind

MY OLD FRIEND Jimmie Connolly, a fine player, used to have trouble playing in the wind. The night before he played a thirty-six-hole match in high wind for the Texas Amateur Championship, he asked me for advice. This is what I told him:

Wind tends to make people hurry. I believe more accidents happen on and off the golf course in March than any other month, because of the wind.

On all shots in the wind, including the putter, pay careful attention to your balance. Do not hurry yourself or your swing. Just be normal. With a driver, tee the ball a little lower against the wind and a little higher when the wind is with you.

Scratch players or pros can hit the old Demaret Quail Shot into the wind, but I don't recommend this shot for the average player. It requires precise timing and a great deal of practice.

Instead, I say if your shot calls for a 5-iron on an ordinary day, into the wind you should hit a 4-iron, or even a 3-iron. The loft on the club will keep the ball low.

If the wind is helping on the same shot, choose a 6-iron, 7-iron, or even an 8-iron.

Remember, the wind is blowing as hard for your opponent as it is for you. Take your time. Keep your balance. Don't let the wind make you hurry or swing hard.

Jimmie Connolly won the state title the next day, 5 and 4.

Titanic Thompson

AUSTIN IS AN EASY drive from Fort Worth, Dallas, San Antonio, and Houston, so naturally our town became a place for traveling hustlers to pause for some action.

Ben Hogan told me about a man named Alvin C. Thomas, later famous as Titanic Thompson, who was hustling in Fort Worth. "He's bound to come through Austin and want to play," Ben said. "He can play left-handed or right-handed, and you can't beat him."

Sure enough, one Sunday afternoon things had slowed down and I was sitting in the golf shop when a stranger walked in and introduced himself. "I am Herman Kaiser from Ardmore, Oklahoma." He showed me his PGA card and asked if he could play our course.

I said that was fine. Kaiser pointed to a big, handsome fellow and said, "This is my amateur friend, Mr. Thomas, a member of my club." As Kaiser and his friend started out the door, Thomas said, "Would you like to play with us?" I said no, I guess not.

They went out on the front nine. One of our members who liked playing for a lot of money came in. I told him about Thomas. The member said, "Harvey, let's catch them on the back side and play them. We'll beat them out of a few hundred. I'll pay if we lose."

So I was out practicing when Thomas and his friend came through. Thomas sat down on a bench. He was wearing a pair of cord shoes, not spikes. I said we'd like to play. Thomas said, "We'll play you all for a dollar a hole, or ten, a hundred, a thousand, you name it." He let us see there was a hole in the sole of his shoe.

I said I'd start off playing the back nine for fifty dollars each, which was a lot of money to me.

We began playing. On the third hole, five or six men in street clothes showed up. They had been playing poker in the clubhouse and came out to see us play golf. Titanic flashed a roll of hundred-dollar bills, and asked if I thought they wanted his money.

On about the sixth hole, Thomas said, "I sure like this place. I think I may stay around for a while." This was shortly before Christmas. Thomas pulled out a little brown candy bag. "You want to give your wife something nice for Christmas?" he said. "Give her a few of these."

The bag was full of diamonds.

I said, no thanks, I guess not.

By the last hole, Thomas and his partner had holed a couple of long putts and beat us 1-up.

In the golf shop afterward, Thomas bought fifty dollars worth of stuff to make up for what I had lost. "I was really lucky today," he told me, the way a hustler would. "You guys nearly had us."

A few months later I saw a picture in the paper of Thomas's partner.

Herman Kaiser's picture was in the paper because he had just won the Masters.

We had many hustlers pass through town.

One big fellow who claimed to be an Indian wanted to play with me using my clubs and him using a slingshot. I took him on. He was very accurate from short range, but he couldn't shoot the ball far enough from the tee with his slingshot to beat me.

Maybe the most bizarre hustlers we ever had were the Duke of Paducah and the Masked Marvel. The Duke was

Austin Country Club, 1914.

selling tickets for a big match of the Masked Marvel against the strongest challenger in town. They decided they wanted to play me for "charity."

We found out why the Marvel wore a mask.

He and the Duke intended to steal the ticket money and escape before the match. We checked up on them and then called off the game and urged them to leave Austin.

Another hustler was hanging around our club trying to get a match when Wilmer Allison walked up and said, "Anybody want to putt against me?"

The hustler's eyes lit up.

"I do," the hustler said. "How much do you want to play for?"

Wilmer said, "The usual—twenty-five cents."

The hustler grabbed his bag and departed to the sound of our laughter.

A Life in Golf

I ONCE HEARD a woman ask, "I wonder how Harvey makes a living? All he does is hang around Austin Country Club."

In a roundabout way I have somehow tried to teach each of my students that golf and life are similar. There's nothing guaranteed to be fair in either golf or life, and we shouldn't expect it to be different.

You must accept your disappointments and triumphs equally.

If you're a pro you may go out there and finish second in the big money, and still you will roll and tumble in bed all night, thinking if you had just made a certain putt or two you would have finished first.

One person can put this kind of thinking behind and go on, but the next one can't and continues tossing and turning, suffering in the mind.

To some it doesn't seem fair that Ben Crenshaw can walk onto a course and just naturally play great golf at the age of twelve, where others might work all their life and never approach being as good.

I played in a lot of tournaments, but I felt that I was playing as much for what I could learn from my fellow pros as for any chance of winning. I knew I wanted to teach, and this was an important part of my learning.

Golf tells you much about character. Play a round of golf with someone, and you know them more intimately than you might from years of dinner parties.

Just watching how close a player steps to the cup when retrieving the ball reveals whether this is a thoughtful, considerate person.

I took care of golf courses for forty years as the superintendent as well as the pro. I used to fight worms. Worms came up through the greens, aerifying them, and as soon as that dirt goes through a worm it's the best fertilizer that could be. But too many worms means too much fertilizer. So we spread a little lye on the greens, turned on the sprinkler, and the worms came tumbling out. We would whip the worms down with a pole and scrape them up with an early-bird rake. We didn't have pesticides. Worms were fine up to a certain point.

We used a spade fork to mash down until you heard the grass pop, aerifying. We would take two men and spend four or five days working from the first to the eighteenth green in the early spring.

Some places put bird boxes around the greens and encouraged birds to move in. When we saw a lot of birds on the greens, we knew we had an insect problem.

When I took the pro job in 1923, Austin Country Club—which was chartered in 1898 as one of the first two golf clubs in Texas—was a sand greens course, as were most courses in the state. We had nine holes until March 2, 1914.

The term "tee box" comes from the box of sand that used to stand at the driving-off places. Players would use the sand to build up little mounds, or tees, to hit the ball off.

In 1924 I convinced the Board to put in grass greens. Austin Muny, where my brother Tom later became the pro, was putting in Bermuda-grass greens, and I argued that we needed them, too.

When we moved the course to Riverside Drive, our architect, Perry Maxwell, put in bent-grass greens. Then we moved to our Pete Dye course in the hills along the lake. I've worn out three courses.

In the old days when they started fertilizing their fairways at Dallas Country Club, Al Badger went over to Fort Worth and got all the cow manure they had at the stockyards. He spread cow manure all over the fairways. This stuff really stunk. Dallas Country Club is in Highland Park, a very ritzy neighborhood. Poor Al took a lot of abuse for that.

If he had used rabbit manure, there wouldn't have been a smell. But how could he have caught enough rabbits, or raided enough hutches, to cover every fairway? Highland Park smelled like cow manure for months.

When they tore down the old courthouse in Austin, they found bat guano three feet deep in the attic. I got an old truck and brought that precious fertilizer back to Austin Country Club. As we drove by the high school in our truck, we passed my daughter, Kathryn, walking home with friends. She pretended not to know me.

I have watched Austin Country Club grow from a nine-

Harvey and Helen Penick, 1981.

hole sand greens course into one of the prettiest, most challenging courses in the country. We have the Colorado River, lakes, canyons, creeks, trees, wildflowers, deer, rabbits, squirrels, birds everywhere.

At first I thought our Pete Dye design might be too difficult for our members. But as our course has matured, our members on all levels of ability have learned to love it as I do. With four tees to each hole, any realistic player can enjoy the game here.

I feel that good bent-grass greens like ours are superior to good Bermuda-grass greens.

If somebody came to me and said, "Harvey, if you had started as a banker when you were a young man, by now you'd be a wealthy retired bank president. Wouldn't that be better than being a retired grown-up caddie?"

If they had said that, and they did, I would answer, "When I was a young man, you didn't become president of a bank unless you were a member of the family that owned it. My oldest brother, Fred, a teller, was the oldest employee of the American Bank. Fred was perfectly satisfied and happy and retired to a two-story home by Onion Creek. But with my ability and my schooling there was no profession anywhere that suited me as much as golf."

The best part of golf is that if you observe the etiquette, you can always find a game. I don't care how good you play, you can find somebody who can beat you, and I don't care how bad you play, you can find somebody you can beat.

The most important thing I can say to any young man or woman who is contemplating a life in golf is this: Marry a good person like I did.

Thank you, Helen.

PART II

---

from
And If You Play Golf, You're My Friend

My Son-in-Law's
First Lesson

My son-in-law, Billy Powell, was captain of the University of Texas basketball team. When my daughter, Kathryn, married him, Billy's pals accused him of trying to improve his golf game.

Everybody knew that was meant as humor, because Billy had never touched a golf club. Basketball was Billy's idea of a real game, not golf.

After college, Billy and Kathryn served a tour in the Air Force. They were stationed at Clovis, New Mexico. Billy tried golf for the first time in Clovis. Playing with a friend who had a 2 handicap, Billy learned what a thrilling experience golf can be. He was hooked.

Billy phoned me that night. He was so excited, he could hardly catch his breath.

"Harvey, I'm on my way to Austin to take a lesson," he said. "How soon can you fit me in?"

I said, "Billy, I will send you a set of golf clubs. Play golf for six months. Then we'll talk about lessons."

Six months later, Billy and I went to the practice range at Austin Country Club.

"I have to ask you a question," Billy said. "I've had an awful struggle for six months. Why did you make me wait so long for this first lesson?"

"This is the second lesson," I said. "Your first lesson was six months of struggle on your own."

"But why?"

I said, "Athletes like you, who have had success in other sports, need to be humbled before they can learn the game of golf."

There's an old saying: The student must be ready for the teacher to appear.

Teaching Billy

I WATCHED MY son-in-law swing at the ball on the practice range for a while without comment. I could tell he wanted me to say something.

Finally I said, "Billy, if you handled your fork the way you do that 7-iron, you would starve to death."

We set the ball on a low tee.

"Now take a swing and just clip off that tee," I said.

He hit behind it. He topped it. He hit it sideways.

I said, "You're a good athlete. Learn to clip off that tee. We can go no further until you do."

I left him alone on the range.

He swung his 7-iron for two days before he learned to clip off the tee.

As our lessons progressed, Billy was eager to reach for the driver. Like everyone, he wanted to boom that ball 250 yards down the fairway. But try as he might, every drive was a slice.

"You'll never get the full enjoyment out of this game hitting a slice," I said. "The only thing that can happen to a slice is, it will get worse."

I took away all his wooden clubs and his long irons. I told him to hit a 4-iron off the tee when he played golf. As soon as he learned to hit a consistent hook off the tee with his 4-iron, we would think about using the wooden clubs.

Months passed. At last Billy's hook was pronounced. He was certain he was ready for the driver. "I can hook my driver now, I believe," he said.

He showed me he could hook it all the way into the trees.

I reminded him that the rough on the left of the fairway is as bad as the rough on the right.

"By the way," I said, "only use your 1-iron when you are in the woods either right or left."

"Why is that, pro?"

"Because you might break it, and then you won't be tempted to use it anymore. I want you to lock your driver, 1-iron, and 2-iron in the closet. Hit your 3-wood off the tee. The more loft you use, the better you will keep the ball in play."

Billy didn't want to hear this, and he didn't obey. He kept trying to hit the ball long distances with his driver. It held his scores back for several years.

Meanwhile, I was constantly trying to help Billy with his putting stroke. Nearly all pupils return to their original sins in the putting game. Billy's original sin was a short back-stroke and a long follow-through.

Every time Billy came to Austin I would say, "Let's see your putting stroke." And there it would be—short back, long through. We would go to the practice green and putt until his back and forward strokes were the same length.

It has been nearly forty summers since the day I gave Billy his "second" lesson, the one that followed his six months of learning humility. Billy became a pretty fair player at Levelland Country Club in west Texas, where he and my daughter, Kathryn, have lived for many years. Billy was the first basketball coach at South Plains College—and the golf coach, as well.

Recently, Billy visited me as I sat under the trees at Austin Country Club on a warm, sunny morning.

"Let me see your stroke for an imaginary two-footer," I said.

You guessed it: Short back, long through.

"Billy, you would have knocked that one off the green," I said. "We better go watch you stroke a few."

A teacher's job is never finished.

A Value of Knowledge

I HEARD BARBARA JORDAN say her grandfather told her that people would reward you, employ you, and pay you if you know how to do something. He encouraged her to learn, and said people would give her an opportunity regardless of color if they respected her knowledge.

As a grown caddie with a high school education, I spent my life learning golf and how to teach it. Barbara Jordan's grandfather was right. People have come to me from all over the world seeking the use of my knowledge, humble though it is.

The Lawyer

HE WAS A LAWYER, about sixty years old, a 14 handicap from another club in town. Over the past thirty years I had given him three or four lessons. Lawyers are not keen on taking lessons. Like engineers and accountants, they want to analyze and complicate everything.

"Harvey, here's my problem," he said. "I've been in a courtroom on a tough case for the last seven weeks. On Saturdays and Sundays, I was reviewing and planning. In preparing for the trial, I worked day and night. This morning, the jury voted for my client."

"Good work," I said.

He nodded. "The problem is, I'm going to Florida to play in a member-guest with an old friend. I haven't touched a golf club in three months. I don't want to embarrass myself or my friend in Florida. Will you watch me hit a few?"

"When does your tournament start?" I asked.

"Tomorrow."

"Tomorrow?"

"I have a flight early in the morning. Our practice-round tee time is 1:47."

I suggested we head for the putting green. "Chipping and putting will get your mind back into the game faster. If you can get up and down for pars a few times in Florida, it will make your friend happy."

"Actually, I'm a pretty good putter," the lawyer said.

On occasions when he had played at our club as a guest, I had heard the lawyer's friends kidding him about his

putting, and not because he was so good at it. We reached the practice green. I selected a level, straight ten-foot putt and asked the lawyer to put down three balls.

The best way to sharpen your putting is to practice with one ball, just as if you are playing that hole on a golf course. But the lawyer was rusty from months away from the game. He needed to get a feel for how far his ball would roll. By using three balls we could see how his touch was adjusting.

"Stop a minute," I said after he had lined up the putt from behind the ball and taken his stance. "Where are you aimed?"

"I don't know."

"Try bringing your right foot back to the line and squaring up."

"I like this open putting stance. I feel more comfortable," he said.

And he knocked that first ball straight into the cup.

"See? I can see the line better with my shoulders open."

"Hit me another," I said.

The second putt missed the hole by inches and went twelve feet past. The third putt was two feet short and wide right. This lawyer didn't have any touch at all on this day. His putting stance was so open—maybe he thought he was copying Raymond Floyd, but it was so exaggerated that it had become a burlesque—that it allowed him no real conception of where his putter was aimed.

We fetched my briefcase and set it on the green, handle up, directly along the line of the putt.

"Please stand square to my briefcase," I asked. "Make some practice strokes. I want the toe of your putter to brush my briefcase. But don't scratch the leather."

"This feels so awkward," he said.

That is always the reaction of a person who plays from an open stance and doesn't understand what square is. "Now let's try it with a ball," I said.

He made two out of three putts, just by my briefcase forcing him to keep his putter face square. Not scratching the leather gave him something to think about, and that produced a good stroke.

We moved to chipping from the fringe with a 7-iron. It would be best for him to stick with one chipping club for a while. I persuaded him to stand close to the ball, not reach out for it. Play it off his right toe, feet close together. I asked him to pretend he was chipping the ball under a bench. He did all right, so we moved to the practice tee.

As usual, I asked him to bring his 7-iron and his 3-wood.

"Harvey, I need to hit some drivers," he said. "There's some swamps in Florida that I can't carry off the tee with my 3-wood."

I remembered that by using the "clip the tee" and "work by the hour" images with this fellow years ago—once I had squared his hips and shoulders with a touch of my cane—he had begun to hit such beautiful 3-woods that he cried out with joy, and I got goose pimples on my arms.

"We'll come to the driver soon enough," I told him. I didn't tell him that soon enough would not be today. "First, hit me some 7-irons."

The lawyer made a few practice swings, slow and lazy. He looked pretty good. He seemed more interested in his swing looking good than in anything else. He thought so intently about how his backswing and his follow-through looked that he almost forgot the part in between. He forgot about clipping the grass with his practice swings. He forced his swing to look good, and the effort kept him from having good balance.

"That's plenty of practice swings to make for a tournament that starts tomorrow," I said. "Maybe you better start hitting some balls."

With a slow, weak effort he flailed the ball about 100 yards.

"Got to loosen up the grease," he said.

"Let's hit this next one hard," I said.

If anything, the swing was even weaker.

"See that flag down by the rock? Take dead aim on it and hit the ball hard."

He made a nice, smooth, rhythmical swing that was the least powerful movement he had made yet. The ball landed short of the rock that was about 120 yards away. The lawyer's club didn't hit the ground hard enough to take a divot.

"That looked pretty good, didn't it?" the lawyer asked.

"Your swing is so weak, if you had been hitting my foot with that 7-iron you wouldn't have bruised my toe," I said.

A sarcastic tone had crept into my voice. I wish it hadn't; a teacher can say almost anything and not offend if he uses the right tone of voice. I should have laughed as if I were joshing him.

The lawyer was more surprised than offended.

"Why, Harvey, I'm sort of stiff. I'll warm up in a minute. I'm not gonna hit you in the foot to prove it, either."

"I shouldn't have spoken to you like that. Hit the rest of those balls," I said. "I'll just keep quiet."

While the lawyer was gently lofting weak, slicing 7-irons, I slipped away.

I hid behind the bushes at the rear of the practice tee. By peeking through some leaves, I could see the lawyer.

"Where did Harvey go?" the lawyer asked.

"I don't know. Didn't see him leave," a member said.

"Does he often vanish in the midst of a lesson?" asked the lawyer.

"He's been known to do it before, yes," the member said.

The lawyer looked at the pile of balls at his feet. He decided he might as well hit them, no matter if I had disappeared.

I watched him through the bushes for fifteen minutes.

What could I tell this lawyer that would help him play in the tournament in Florida?

He needed to square his hips and shoulders. He needed a stronger grip. He needed to stop his left wrist from breaking down.

Had this pupil been a good player, I could have showed him any or all of these things. But any advice I would give the lawyer about his stance and swing would make him worry about it on the plane, and then he'd overdo everything.

So I went home.

I sat in my chair and thought about the lawyer. There must have been some way I could help him. I believed I had helped his putting stroke. We had kept his hands ahead of the clubhead by chipping low shots under the imaginary bench. As he kept hitting those weak, slicing 7-irons—he called them "fades"—I noticed that he was consistent with them. It was a shot he could count on. A person can build an entire round around one consistent shot.

Finally, about dinner time, I asked Helen to phone the lawyer.

"Hello, this is Helen Penick," she said. "Harvey asked me to call. He can't hear well enough to talk on the phone, you know. Well, he has been sitting here for hours thinking about you. And he said for me to tell you this—go to Florida and have a good time, you'll do just fine."

Two weeks later he came by the club to see me. He was a happy lawyer. He and his friend had won their flight, and he had shot his handicap. He thanked me for helping him tune up his swing.

I should have thanked *him*—for reminding me that it's not what the teacher says, but what the student hears that matters.

God Knows

GOD MADE WHAT is called the lifeline in the right palm of a human being for one very special reason . . .

It fits just exactly perfectly against the left thumb in a good golf grip.

In the Mind's Eye

BARBARA PUETT APPROACHED me one fine spring morning with a problem that was confounding her.

"Harvey, I'm hitting it fat," she said. "No matter how I adjust, I keep hitting behind the ball. I'm desperate. Please tell me what's gone wrong with my swing."

Barbara was one of my better pupils. She used to play round after round with young Tommy Kite. By the time Barbara came to see me with this "fat" problem, she had become a golf teacher herself.

"Let me watch you hit a few 7-irons, Barbara," I said.

She made a few swings. Sure enough, she hit behind the ball every time. Barbara's address position looked fine. She was too good a player to be doing this.

"Let's not use a ball," I said. "I want you to pick out a spot on the ground, a leaf or a piece of grass, and hit that spot."

"I'll try," Barbara said.

Harvey in his office, c. 1950.

She would select a leaf or a twig or a tuft and swing at it—and her 7-iron would dig into the ground behind it. Barbara was growing very upset.

"What's wrong with my swing, Harvey?" she pleaded.

"I can't say," I said.

"Why?"

"Barbara, after all the years you've spent practicing and playing golf, if you can't hit a spot on the ground with your swing, there is nothing I can do to help you. Go home. Go out in your backyard. Keep swinging your 7-iron at a spot on the ground. When you hit that spot regularly, come back and see me—if you need to."

The next time I saw Barbara she had just finished a round of golf and turned in a good score. She was excited.

"You cured yourself," I said.

"I went to my backyard like you said. I started swinging at a spot," she said, grinning, "and suddenly it came to me.

"There was nothing wrong with my swing. If I couldn't hit a spot, it was because my mind wasn't on it. Once I quit thinking about my swing and really put my mind onto hitting a spot, the problem went away."

Flavor That Lasts

IF YOU WERE asked to imagine what flavor of ice cream would describe your golf swing, I would like to hear you answer, "vanilla."

The more simple your approach to the swing is, the better off you are. It's the simple things that last.

A Story by Helen

THE TELEPHONE RINGS frequently in the kitchen of our home near Austin Country Club.

Unless one of Harvey's day nurses get the phone while I'm shopping or playing cards—I love bridge and gin rummy—I'm the one who answers.

Harvey sits in his favorite chair in the living room beyond the open kitchen door. He is about twenty feet from the phone. But Harvey hasn't been able to walk for several years now, and his hearing is poor. It is a terrible strain for him to try to talk on the phone.

As a result, I have become the translator between Harvey and his callers.

You can't believe some of the calls 1 have answered.

I have given putting lessons to golf pros on the phone, shouting their questions to Harvey.

All sorts of people phone Harvey, from golf pros to average players to fans and friends and those who are just plain curious.

Recently I picked up the phone and heard a man say, "Put Harvey Penick on the line, please."

I explained about Harvey's problem with the phone.

"Well, you tell him I am coming to see him for a week of lessons," the man said.

"I don't know if Harvey will be able to see you," I said. "Especially not for a whole week. It's a bit too hard on him."

"What's hard about it?"

I said, "Harvey is getting along in years, you know."

"He is, is he?" the man said. "You tell him to fire up and get ready to teach. I'm leaving in a few minutes, driving down there from Sacramento."

I said, "I'm afraid you are wasting your time."

The man said, "Nope, I have no time to waste. You see, I am ninety years old myself."

I'm sure Harvey will see him, but the man hasn't arrived. I hope his time didn't run out while he was on his way.

An Irony

IN GOLF YOUR strengths and weaknesses will always be there. If you could improve your weaknesses, you would improve your game.

The irony is that people prefer to practice their strengths.

The First Choice

WHEN YOU ARE trying to decide which club to hit, the first one that comes to mind is the right one.

Let us suppose your instinct tells you to pull a 5-iron out of the bag.

Your instinct is correct. Hit the 5-iron.

But you throw up some grass to test the wind and you

check the yardage again, and you overrule your instinct. You change to a 4-iron, or maybe to a 6-iron.

Now you are no longer sure. You'll probably ease up on the 4-iron or really bear down on the 6-iron. The result is liable to be a poor shot.

Go ahead and hit the club your inner voice first tells you to hit. If your judgment is a little off, so what? It's only a few yards' difference between clubs.

The important difference is in confidence.

Confidence is contagious.

A Strange World

CALL ME OLD-FASHIONED or starchy or whatever you will, but two things in this world I just can't grow accustomed to are a man and a woman living together without being married—and taking a mulligan at golf.

Look Here First

NINE OUT OF ten problems with the swing of the average golfer begin with the grip or the stance.

The symptoms that come from these two sources are many and various.

It is easy for teachers to get caught up in treating the

symptoms without first going to the underlying causes in the grip and the stance.

Higher Aspects

PEOPLE SAY TO me that golf is a *spiritual* game. I don't believe I understand how that word applies to golf. According to my dictionary, the first meaning of "spiritual" is "Of the spirit or the soul as distinguished from the body."

It is true that golf is a game in which you seem to get in touch with higher parts of yourself. We can say golf is spiritual in that respect. But we can't leave the body out of the golf swing, can we?

All my life I have been asking people what the difference is between faith and confidence.

One of my pupils told me, "Confidence is that feeling I get just before I learn better."

Another said, "Confidence in golf is when I am faced with a certain shot that I have hit successfully many times, and I know full well I will do it again. Faith is when I may never have hit this particular shot before, but I trust that I can do it because I have faith in my swing."

Most people say faith is religious, but they feel that confidence is something different.

My dictionary says faith is "Unquestioning belief in God, religion, or a system of religious beliefs."

Confidence, according to my dictionary, is "Firm belief in the truth or reality of a fact, or trust and reliance on one's own abilities."

It seems to me that confidence is the feeling we want to

have in playing golf. But we can't dismiss the value of faith, either.

I think faith is in the heart, and confidence is in the mind.

A Method for Madness

A FRIEND WROTE me a letter from Sawgrass Country Club in Ponte Vedra, Florida.

He wanted to know, "How can I keep from getting so insanely mad on the golf course? I know losing my temper is not good for my game. But when I blow a short putt and then hook a drive into the marsh, I go crazy with anger and despair. Then things get rapidly worse. I know it's stupid to get mad but what can I do?"

I think it is fine to get mad if you hit a poor shot or miss a putt you should have made. Getting mad shows you have the competitive spirit. They call him "Gentle Ben" Crenshaw, but he's always had flashes of temper on the course because he wants to win and he wants to be the best.

So get mad. But do it in a gentlemanly way.

In your mind call yourself every name you can think of for the poor shot you just hit.

But while you are being mad, be mad only at yourself.

Do not be mad at your clubs or the golf course. They're the same as they were when you hit a great shot yesterday. And don't be mad at luck. Stick to the one thing you can control: you.

Then forget it. Cast the bad names out of your mind and be thinking positively by the time you approach your next shot. Your next shot is a new experience. It might be the best shot you ever hit in your life.

A Distinction

———

THE ABILITY TO concentrate is good, but thinking too much about how you are doing what you are doing is disastrous.

Trust your muscles and hit the ball to the hole. Keep it simple.

From the Fringe

———

ON A PAR FOUR, if your ball is on the fringe of the green in two strokes and you require three more strokes to get into the hole, you might as well have whiffed your tee shot.

The penalty is the same—the loss of one stroke.

If you whiffed your tee shot, you would be embarrassed. But if you take three from the fringe, you are apt to say, "Well, that's just my game."

You should feel that you can get down in two from the fringe every time. Practice it. There's no use throwing away all those strokes.

The Lay Up

ONE OF THE WORST shots in golf is when a player decides to lay up short of a hazard and yet hits enough club to reach the trouble—and usually does.

Often this is because the player chooses a club that will land as close as possible short of the hazard. He hits it easy, he thinks. But his easy swing catches the ball solid and it goes ten yards farther than usual.

If you are laying up, be sure you lay up and not in.

You might think of the shot as "laying back" from the hazard, rather than "laying up" to the edge of it.

Tommy Wins the Open

ON THE FINAL day of the 1992 U.S. Open at Pebble Beach, with the wind and rain howling in off the ocean, Tommy Kite played one of the finest, most courageous rounds of golf in the history of the game.

Sitting in front of my television back home in Austin, I was so moved and so proud of Tommy that my toes curled up and I cried like a baby when they put the championship trophy in his hands at the end of that excruciating day.

When Tommy came by to visit with me sometime later, I

asked what he had been thinking about during the hours he was battling horrible weather conditions to emerge as champion over the best players in the world.

I have always impressed on my pupils that when they're playing in the wind and rain and cold, they should take their time. I don't mean play slow. I mean just don't hurry.

So it warmed my heart when Tommy said, "I was thinking, 'Take your time.'"

I asked him to tell me about it.

"In a situation like that," he said, "with players being blown away, somehow you've got to forget about your swing or any mechanical thoughts and get into a really trusting mentality.

"You just have to take the attitude that you have done all the training that is required, and if you're not going to trust it, why do all the training?"

He got that line from sports psychologist Dr. Bob Rotella. I love that line. Trust it.

"I use that thought an awful lot when I'm on the golf course and have a chance to win the tournament," Tommy said. "I keep telling myself to trust it, just go ahead and trust it.

"There's no point in training and working hard if when you get out there on the golf course or the football field or whatever, you're not going to trust the fact that you know how to do it. Like Troy Aikman. He trusts himself to throw the football where he wants to put it. Otherwise, why should he bother with all that practice?

"As for taking my time, I mean I want to be totally ready to play the shot before I play the shot. I must be 100 percent committed to playing this particular shot at this particular moment. In bad weather, if it takes a little longer to get ready, then I need to take a little longer."

We remembered one year at the Masters when Ben

Crenshaw was preparing to hit his approach shot to the seventy-second hole. Ben needed a birdie to win his second Masters or a par to get into a playoff. It was raining. Ben's glove was wet. He missed the green, made a bogey on the hole, and finished second.

"Ben just got into a little bit of a rush," Tommy said. "It would only have taken a minute for him to reach in his bag and pull out a brand-new dry glove right out of a package and feel good about it.

"It was kind of like he was thinking, well, you know, it's okay, I can hit this shot anyway. And then when you miss it, you're kicking yourself in the rear all the way.

"Lee Trevino made the comment, 'I don't care if you have to send your caddie into the pro shop to buy a new glove. When you've got the Masters laying on the line, you don't hit the ball until you are ready.' I'm not picking on Ben when I say this, because I've done dumb things like that way too often.

"When I woke up Sunday morning at the Open and stepped outside and felt the wind and rain in my face, I knew I had an excellent chance to win if I just took my time and trusted myself."

Tommy took dead aim that day.

A Story by Christy Kite

AFTER TOM WON the Open on Sunday, he was supposed to play an outing in St. Louis the next day. Monterey, California, is not the easiest place in the world to get out of, so I decided I would fly to St. Louis with him and then fly home to

Austin on Monday morning rather than spending the night by myself in Monterey.

They had two private planes waiting to take us to St. Louis. Most people took the earlier one. The only people on the later plane were Craig Stadler and us.

The plane was delayed, so Craig went to dinner. We were waiting for him to come back. Now it was just Tom and I on the plane, and we had the U.S. Open Trophy with us.

Tom said, "You'll be flying home tomorrow, but the first thing Tuesday morning, I want you to take this trophy over to Mr. Penick and set it right in his lap."

Tuesday morning, I took the trophy to Austin Country Club, where Mr. Penick was giving a lesson to a woman who had come down from Rhode Island to see him.

I walked up to his golf cart and said, "Mr. Penick, this is for you."

I put the U.S. Open Trophy in his lap.

I said, "Tom said a big piece of this trophy belongs to you."

Mr. Penick started crying. I started crying. Pretty soon all the people around his cart were crying and laughing at the same time.

I wish Tom could have been there to give Mr. Penick the trophy himself, but he couldn't, and I did it the way Tom wanted me to do it. It was a great pleasure, that's for sure.

Make Up Your Mind

ON EVERY KIND of golf shot, you must make up your mind exactly what it is you want to do. Do not have the slightest doubt. As a friend of mine says of the way he lives his life, "I may be wrong, but I am never in doubt."

If there is doubt in your mind over a golf shot, how can your muscles know what they are expected to do?

What most average players can't seem to grasp is that this is just as true of a two-foot putt as it is of any other shot.

Watching the Bob Hope Tournament on television one Saturday, I saw Tommy Kite coming down the stretch miss a putt that was so short, he could easily have kicked it in.

The television commentator said Tommy's stroke broke down. Well, I could see that it wasn't a great stroke, but I doubted if mechanics had anything to do with missing the putt.

On Sunday, Tommy holed everything he looked at, shot a course record, and won the tournament going away at 35 under par.

When he came home, I asked him about that putt he missed on Saturday.

"I'd had the same putt in a practice round," he said. "The green back there has so much slope to it that it looks like it breaks off the world. When I stood over the putt in the tournament, I was thinking it was just outside the right edge of the hole. But I looked again and thought, whoa, I'm playing too much break. I know it breaks a lot, but, gosh, does it break this much?

"Instead of stepping back and starting over with a clear mind, I stroked the putt and missed it. Missing the putt had nothing to do with the stroke. I missed it because I wasn't thinking right. I wasn't ready to play the shot.

"Sunday I knew I was going to putt well. All I did was make up my mind I would be totally committed to every stroke."

If this is what is required of the U.S. Open champion, how can the average golfer expect to get by with less?

The California Woman

I WAS GIVING a lesson to a woman from California who already had a pretty good game, but wanted to lower her handicap to a single number.

Something was wrong.

She was hitting the ball decently, but she kept frowning and fidgeting.

After half an hour she said, "Harvey, what you are telling me is too simple. It is so simple that I can't understand it."

It wasn't the first time I have been criticized for being too simple, nor was it the last.

Some pupils are not happy unless the teacher gives them plenty of technical talk to chew on. They want the teacher to fill their minds with "golf-swing theory."

These pupils leave me and move on to other, smarter teachers.

No hard feelings on my part.

From my point of view, I don't teach theory. I teach simple things that produce good results.

The woman from California said, "I don't understand what you mean by 'clip off the tee.'"

"But you've been doing it," I said. "Are you unhappy with the results?"

"No, the results are fine. What I want to know is *why* the results are fine."

"Because when you clip off the tee you square your clubface," I said.

"I know that," she said. "But *why* does it square my clubface?"

*Harvey with Sandra Palmer, Ben Crenshaw,
and Tom Kite, 1993.*

"It's natural," I said.

"That's not a good enough answer," she said.

A few days earlier, the touring pro Tommy Aaron had come to the club for a lesson. I watched him hit balls all afternoon. At the end he said, "Well, what's the answer?"

I said, "You hit the ball beautifully. Ball-striking is not the reason you aren't winning."

"So what is the reason?" he asked.

"I don't know," I said.

That was not the answer Tommy wanted, but it was honest.

The woman from California stuck her club back in the bag, peeled off her glove, and said, "You make it sound too easy. My husband is the one you ought to be teaching. He's dumb enough to understand you. What do I owe you for this lesson?"

"Nothing," I said.

"You can't mean that."

"How could I charge you money for not helping you?" I said.

"But this is embarrassing. I must pay you for your time."

She left angry that I wouldn't take her money. There's no pleasing some people.

The Judge

HE WAS A JUDGE from out of town.

His overlapping stomach presented the judge with a dilemma. If he stood where he could see the ball, he couldn't reach it. If he stood where he could hit the ball, he couldn't see it.

After five lessons in a week, I had done very little to improve the judge's golf swing. But he was preparing to return home, and I wanted to give him at least one positive thought.

"Judge," I said, "I have a suggestion that will help make your game more fun."

"What is it?" he asked.

"Always play with clean golf balls."

Keep It Moving

POOR PLAYERS USUALLY seem embarrassed to play with good players.

The fact is that you may not be good enough to play with the good players, but no one will notice if you keep up.

The good players are not going to be watching you and criticizing your swing. They have their own games to deal with.

But if you hold up play, the others will notice you—and probably not in a kindly manner.

If you, as a poor player, lose your temper along with your golf balls, and shout and throw clubs and curse your luck, and plumb-bob all your putts from both sides of the hole, the good players will be disgusted. They'll avoid you for the rest of your life, not only on the golf course, but in the social and business worlds as well.

So just keep the game moving in a good humor, and you will always be welcome.

The True Way

I WAS WATCHING four of my University of Texas players getting ready to hit on the first tee one afternoon in the early spring.

They were discussing whether to play "winter" rules or "summer" rules.

"What do you think, Coach?"

I said, "Well, you boys can go play golf. Or else you can make up some other game and go play that, instead."

They understood my meaning.

In the game of golf, the ball is played as you find it.

A Special Club

IF SOMEONE GIVES you a driver, it might be wise to ask yourself, Why?

I never knew of a player to give away a driver he could hit really well.

For most everyone, the driver is the most difficult club in the bag. I have seen Arnold Palmer bring drivers into the workshop half a dozen at a time and file and whittle and scrape in an effort to get a club that felt just right to him. The next day he might be back with half a dozen more. When a player finds a driver he falls in love with, he keeps it forever—or at least until he falls out of love and divorces the club and sends it to live with eight or ten other drivers in the closet or the trunk of the car.

People are even stranger about their drivers than about their putters, as a rule.

I remember how in about 1962 a manufacturer came out with a new driver that had some kind of a slot in the head that supposedly increased distance. One of my Texas boys, Billy Munn, told me he wanted to buy the new driver.

I said, "I didn't realize you had broken your old driver, Billy. Let's see if we can fix it."

There was nothing wrong with Billy's old driver, and he was good with it. Like all golfers, Billy was being gullible to the lure of advertising.

Byron Nelson tells a story that illustrates how players feel about their drivers.

In the middle 1930s, when he was a struggling young pro, Byron told his wife, Louise, that he needed to dig into their meager supply of money to buy a new driver.

Louise said, "Byron, since we've been married I haven't bought a new dress or a new pair of shoes, but in the past year you have bought four new drivers.

"Either you don't know what kind of driver you want, or else you don't know how to drive."

The next morning Byron took one of his drivers into the shop, working on it until it felt good in his hands, and played with it for a long time.

A Golfer's Prayer

DEAR GOD,
    In the annals of time
    a handful of citizens stood
    at the edge of a pasture.
With crooks in hand and stones about
    they made the first drives
    that one day would evolve into golf.

Just one of those first drivers had talent,
    and the rest were only determined.
That one talented driver drove the rest
    to lives of dedication, though often
    mediocrity and despair.

Grant us, O Lord, the grace to use the
    clubs you have blessed us with,
The disposition not to cloud
    our judgment and stance.

We beseech you, Lord, to heal our slice,
    to straighten our hook, to carve our
    divots truly, to improve our lie,
    making it just a tad better than our opponent's.

from *And If You Play Golf, You're My Friend* • 159

Give us the vision to keep our eye
   on the ball, our grip uncomfortable
   enough to be true, our minds and hearts
   pure as the course we play.

We ask this in Your Name.

   Amen.

—Monsignor Richard E. McCabe
   at Caritas Charity Dinner
   Austin, Texas, November 24, 1992

Give Luck a Chance

DAVIS LOVE III had been playing on the tour for a while, and everyone could see he had a world of talent as well as a wonderful swing that he had been taught by his father, Davis, Jr., who was one of my University of Texas boys.

But Davis III had not won a tournament. So his dad brought him to me to see if I might have some idea that would help.

I watched Davis III hit some shots. He hit that ball like it was coming out of a cannon. It flew so fast and so far that I couldn't even follow it with my eyes.

But I could see well enough to follow his swing, of course. I made a few small suggestions. Nothing much. Then we went to the practice green.

Harvey with Davis Love, Jr. (front seat),
Ed Turley, and Davis Love III (rear).

Davis III set up fifteen feet from the hole and started stroking putts.

Oh my. Now I did see something I don't like.

Unless they hit the cup and rattled in, all those putts were going two or three feet past the hole.

I have always said that one of the worst sayings in golf is "Never up, never in."

Helen Dettweiler said that saying should be, "Always up, never in!"

Bobby Jones made the point that while a putt left short of the hole obviously didn't go in, neither did a putt that went past the hole. And there are many more three-putts coming back from beyond the cup than there are from just short of it.

After watching Davis III putt for a while, I said, "Son, I want you to try to get that ball to die somewhere around the hole. Work on your speed, your touch. Just roll the ball up there near the hole, and they'll start falling in. The idea is not to try to make every putt from this distance. You want to roll the ball to die at the hole."

I saw him thinking about it.

I said, "If you keep rolling the ball to die at the hole, you give luck a chance to happen."

A couple of weeks later, Davis III was on the seventeenth hole at Harbour Town with a thirty-foot putt. He sank it and won the tournament.

His excited father phoned me that night.

Davis, Jr., said, "He told me, 'Dad, I did exactly what Mr. Penick was talking about. I rolled it up there and gave luck a chance to happen—and it did.'"

A Teacher's Guide

IN 1929, MY sixth year as head pro, I pulled a pencil and a black ledger book out of a drawer in the golf shop and wrote for myself what could be called a guide to my thinking and behavior as a teacher and as a person.

I don't claim to be the creator of these principles. They are at least as old as the Bible. But I didn't write them in the black ledger book because I had learned them in Sunday school. I wrote them because I needed to use them in my everyday life.

This guide grew out of my experience as a caddie and shop manager and teacher. It is common sense. If it's so simple, why did I need to write it in the ledger in 1929?

In the midst of a lesson with a stubborn pupil that day, I found myself saying harshly, "I wish your brain and muscles were as coordinated as the clothes you're wearing!"

The look of hurt on the pupil's face caused me to apologize. I told him he was making progress and we would resume the lesson another day, by which time I would be a better teacher.

I walked into the golf shop, pulled out the ledger, and wrote the simple guide that I tried to follow for the rest of my life.

Like golf instruction, these principles are easy to learn, but useless unless they are put into action.

And like golf instruction, these principles are easy to forget. I need to read them every few days.

This is what I wrote:

Criticize yourself once in a while and see what you may be doing wrong. Never criticize others. It only stirs resentment. Speak no *ill* of anyone and *all* the good you know of everyone. Don't judge a person too soon. God waits until the end.

All people like to be important. Criticism from a teacher can kill the pupil's ambition to improve. Be anxious to praise and slow on fault-finding.

Nations and peoples also feel their importance. A top Eskimo feels superior to a Vanderbilt. Most people you meet feel superior to you in some way. Let them know you realize their importance, but avoid flattery.

Emerson said, "Everyone is my superior in some way." In that knowledge, I learn from them.

The best way to get pupils to do something is to get them to want to do it. Try to make the other person happy about doing something you suggest.

"Don't argue!" Even if you win, you usually lose your pupil's goodwill.

———

Don't tell pupils they are wrong. Most of us are prejudiced about ourselves. When we are wrong, we may admit it to ourselves—but not if someone is trying to force the "facts" down our throats.

———

I never know so much that I can't learn more.

———

Don't make direct contradictions to the sentiments of pupils combined with positive assertions of your own. Don't say, "Certainly, undoubtedly." Say, "I believe; I conceive; it appears at present; in some cases it might be right, but in the present case there seems to me some difference."

———

When I am at fault, simply say I am at fault and there is no excuse for it. I will do better next time, or at least I will change it.

———

Be friendly. Forget yourself. Stop thinking about "I." Listen to other people, keep interested in everyone else—caddies and members and all. Find out what they are doing and what they care about.

Try and remember names.

Try and talk plain.

A pro, or anyone, either goes forward or backward. What am I doing?

Try and be simple in living as well as in teaching or playing. The long odds are against us if we shoot the hard way.

Life consists of a lot of minor annoyances and few matters of real consequence.

We are frequently misjudged by our superiors, but never by our subordinates.

A stout heart usually accompanies a soft-spoken voice.

Finish one job well before starting another.

———

Listen to the kicks from anyone. You usually know the people and if they really have a kick coming.

———

Instead of doing what is right and best, we are influenced by associates. I must be an influence and example to members, caddies, and friends.

———

Always smile when you give anything, no matter how much it hurts. This means when giving service or anything else.

———

Be brave if you lose and meek if you win.

———

A good way to size up a person is to hear him say what he thinks it takes "guts" to do. A robber thinks it takes guts to do a daring job. A doctor thinks it takes guts to do a risky operation. A preacher probably believes it takes guts to tell his people to live according to the teachings of Jesus. The congregation will criticize him for it.

———

Teaching is a teacher's best advertisement. Caddies are good advertisers. They will watch you and copy you if they see that your teaching is good.

Practically all of the awkwardness and odd ways people have are an outgrowth of misunderstanding some of the few simple fundamentals.

I hear lots of shortcuts to par golf. But the only way to get there is with hard practice, sound style, and thought. I try to teach a pupil to swing the club correctly. The pupil must learn to hit the ball with that swing and get it in the hole.

Don't play too much golf or gamble at cards with the members. Call people "Mister" and "Mrs." and make sure your assistants do the same. Stay away from the social angles of the club.

When I go to a doctor, all I ask is for him to have my interest at heart. I try to do that as a teacher. First of all, a teacher must try to understand what is going on in the pupil's mind. The teaching must be simple. Don't get technical. Put yourself in the pupil's place.

Wilmer's Woes

WILMER ALLISON, GREAT tennis player and coach, was devoted to the game of golf.

Late one afternoon, we were playing and we came to a par five. Wilmer hit a good drive down the middle. He hit a nice second shot right up in front of the green, just a short pitch away.

Wilmer shanked the pitch shot.

He walked around behind the bunker to play his next shot, and he shanked it again. Now he was almost in back of the green as he set up for another pitch shot.

Again he shanked it.

This put Wilmer to the left of the green. He took a couple of practice swings, set up for his pitch—and shanked it again.

Four shanks in a row took Wilmer on a complete circle of the green and placed him back in the middle of the fairway.

We were all laughing—all except Wilmer, I mean—as he pulled out his putter and banged the ball onto the putting surface.

"Well, after all, Wilmer, it is the shank of the evening," someone said when we reached the next tee.

You can imagine where Wilmer's drive went.

The Champion

NOT ONLY DOES Mickey Wright have one of the best—many would argue that it is the *very* best—golf swings in history, she is one of the classiest people it has ever been my privilege to know as a friend and pupil.

When she was asked at age fifty-eight why she had chosen to live a quiet life rather than cashing in on her many titles and her Hall-of-Fame status, Mickey said:

"I have no interest in translating my name into a million dollars, or any amount. To me golf means one thing and always has: the pure pleasure I get from swinging a golf club."

Practice It First

WHEN DARRELL ROYAL was coaching our football team at the University of Texas, he wouldn't have called upon his boys to run a play that they had never practiced in a game.

I believe the golfer should never try to play a shot he hasn't practiced a good deal.

On a windy day, most average golfers will go out and try to hit a low ball into the wind, or a high ball with the wind, when in the course of regular events they never practice either of those shots.

The only time most average golfers try to hit a soft, high

wedge over a bunker is when they are faced with this predicament during a round of golf. You don't see many average golfers out there practicing with their wedges.

Much better for you to learn different shots on the practice range rather than banging away at the same one hour after hour.

I do advise, however, that average golfers select one club, perhaps a 7-iron, and learn to love it like a sweetheart. Learn how far it goes. Learn to hit it high or low, to hook it or slice it.

An average golfer can build a decent game around one club.

Wrongheaded Husbands

ONE OF THE BIGGEST problems with women golfers is their husbands.

A husband nearly always tells his wife she "raised up."

This unfortunate woman will try her best to "stay down." But she can't hit the ball from there. She will hit the ground in back of it, or her left arm will bend at impact.

The most common reason for raising up is consciously trying to stay down. You can't raise up unless you are down to begin with.

The woman should be thinking, "chin up, stand tall"— not "stay down."

It pains me to hear the terrible advice husbands constantly give their wives regarding golf.

For years, her husband loudly admonished Joan Whitworth, one of my favorite women pupils, to "keep your head still." He got her so locked up that I could hardly persuade her to make a free swing. Joan is a fine athlete, too. What a pity her husband, Harry, didn't keep his golfing wisdom to himself.

Children

I DON'T TRY to teach golf to children. What they need is someone who will guide their learning. Let them play, then help them when they want you to, or when you see something that demands a teacher's attention.

Hit It Hard

VERY EARLY IN our time together I try to get my pupils to hit the ball hard, even with the short irons.

I believe if you start off in the game hitting the ball easy, you generally will keep it up. Your muscles learn the slow pace. You will always lack distance.

Sometimes it takes longer to unlearn than it does to learn.

How to Stop the Bleeding

ALL GOOD PLAYERS reach patches in the midst of rounds when their games go awry.

I'm not talking about the habitual Erratics. I mean consistent, good players who for no apparent reason start making a string of bogeys, maybe a double bogey or two. They call it "bleeding." They ask me, "How can I stop the bleeding?"

As I always say of good players, you don't lose your swing between the green and the next tee, or between the tee and the approach shot.

The bleeding may be caused by bad breaks, which you simply must cope with. You should make birdies with your good breaks, but your bad breaks must not be allowed to mess up your thinking and poison your attitude.

Leaving breaks out of it, what causes the bleeding is what is going on in your mind during that five or ten minutes between shots.

While walking from your drive to your approach, is your mind caught up in considering results? Are you thinking ahead to future holes? For example, perhaps you are thinking, "I'll knock this wedge stiff for a birdie, then par that long, hard hole, reach the seventeenth in two for a cinch birdie—and par on the final hole will pay me a great, big fat check!"

Not only are you living too far in the future to be playing a sharp game of golf, you have let the thought of gold enter your mind. There may be gold and riches awaiting you, but not if you have started dreaming about them. You reach your reward stroke by stroke. You must be mindful of each stroke as it is played. Golf is played in the present.

If you can wash your mind clean each time while walking to your next shot, you have the makings of a champion.

That's what I mean by taking dead aim. I mean clearing the mind of all thoughts except the thought of the target, so that the muscles are free to do the job.

A good player's muscles do what they are told to do if they are free to do it.

Now let's suppose you are struggling with getting your mind on the job at hand, but nothing helps. You just can't do it. You can't stop the bleeding. What do you do?

You take it to the Lord in prayer—that is my best answer.

The Dashing Demaret

AT OUR ORIGINAL Austin Country Club—the first of our three locations—the dashing young Jimmy Demaret walked into the shop one day and asked me to play a round with him.

"I'm working on something in my swing. Let's go see how I'm doing with it," he said.

In later years, as he went on to win three Masters championships, Jimmy became a little plump and was famous for his colorful style of dressing, which attracted many fans to the game.

But on the day I am speaking of, Jimmy was thin and wiry, with big, strong forearms and powerful hands. I had powerful hands myself, from years of grinding and buffing clubs, but I wasn't as strong as Jimmy by any means.

Jimmy Demaret. Harvey taped this photo to his office window to demonstrate the perfect follow-through.

Jimmy also was one of the most handsome fellows ever born and had a quick wit that stood him well in the company of such wits as Bob Hope and Bing Crosby.

Even as a young man, my face had already begun to wrinkle from sun and wind and, I suppose, something in my genes. Jimmy used to say, "Harvey, I could pour a bucket of water on your head, and not a drop of it would reach the ground."

Anyhow, Jimmy and I set out for a round of golf on the original Austin Country Club course.

"What is it you are trying to do with your swing?" I asked him on the tee.

He said, "I am trying to keep my elbows out in front of me on my follow-through."

I watched his swing intently that day, but I didn't get to see it very often.

Jimmy shot 30–29—59.

Ever since, keeping the elbows out in front on the follow-through has been one of the things I emphasize in teaching.

Wasting Your Time

UNLESS YOU HAVE a reasonably good grip and stance, anything you read about the golf swing is useless.

Fate Takes a Hand

IT WAS A CRISP morning in May, and the Southwest Conference golf championship was on the line.

As the University of Texas coach, I sent my four best players—Morris Williams, Jr., Marion Pfluger, Wesley Ellis, and Billy Penn—to Fort Worth to play undefeated TCU at one of the finest golf courses in the world, Colonial Country Club.

From its inception Colonial has been rated the top course in Texas, or very close to it. But in the days of this match I am about to describe, Colonial was even tougher than it is today. Storms and floods have destroyed many of Colonial's giant oaks, and architectural decisions have pulled some of the teeth that the original designer, my friend John Bredemus, put into the layout.

I am not diminishing the Colonial of today. It is a great course. But forty years ago—when Colonial was known as Hogan's Alley—it was tighter and harder than it is now.

My number-one player, Morris Williams, Jr., had lost only one match in his life. That was when Harvie Ward, the best amateur in the world for ten years, beat Morris l-up in the thirty-six-hole NCAA final in 1949.

Morris had beaten Billy Maxwell, Don January, Earl Stewart, Don Cherry, Joe Conrad, Buster Reed, and the Cupit brothers, among others, during his brief career that was to be ended soon in a plane crash.

We needed to win at Colonial to assure Texas another SWC title. So I matched Morris against the TCU captain, a tall, slender, cocky sophomore named Dan Jenkins.

This Jenkins boy was not only a full-time student at TCU, he was also a full-time sportswriter for *The Fort Worth Press*.

From the tips Colonial played more than seven thousand yards and looked twice as long. As a concession to the members, who were generous to allow college teams to compete there, the TCU and Texas squads started on the back nine first.

Morris had never seen Colonial, but he later told me that Jenkins, with whom he had become friendly, was nice enough to point out every danger and pitfall that Morris might have overlooked.

On the tee Jenkins would say, "You want to stay left here . . . a creek comes in over there . . . this next green is slick as a glacier."

No doubt Jenkins was trying to mess up Morris's mind. But that sort of needling never worked with Morris. With his pants cuffs turned up a couple of times, and a repeating upright swing, Morris almost never missed a fairway or green. When Morris had a 9-iron or wedge in his hand, he expected to hit it stiff. Morris played with incredible confidence, the kind that comes from knowing you'll have to be under par to beat him. Morris was grinning and friendly, almost apologetic about how good he was.

After fifteen holes Williams and Jenkins were even par and level in the match.

Ben Hogan and Marvin Leonard, the mercantile king whose imagination and money built Colonial, drove up in a golf cart to watch them.

Morris was greatly impressed. He asked Dan, "Does Hogan follow you guys much?"

"Oh, sure, all the time," Jenkins said.

At Colonial's seventh hole—the sixteenth of their match—Jenkins pushed a 1-iron off the tee into the right rough behind some trees. Morris hit a 3-wood down the middle.

Jenkins had a shot if he could hook a high 6-iron over the trees and hit it far enough to reach the green. With Hogan watching, Jenkins hit perhaps the best shot he would ever hit in his life. The ball came to rest six inches from the cup for a cinch birdie. This birdie would have put Jenkins 1-up on Morris with two holes to play.

From back down the fairway, Morris pulled out a 7-iron, settled into that square stance of his—and hit the ball into the cup for an eagle!

Deeply shaken, Jenkins three-putted the next hole and lost the match, 2 and 1.

Texas had won another championship. Morris shot a 68, two under par, the one and only time he ever saw Colonial.

One year later in the Southwest Conference Tournament—a medal event that was played to establish the individual champion—this same Jenkins kid three-putted sixteen times in seventy-two holes to finish third behind Buddy Weaver of Rice and Wesley Ellis of Texas.

Over the years, I have come to know Dan Jenkins as a friend as well as a famous sportswriter and novelist.

I like to tell him, "Well, Dan, think how lucky you are. If Morris hadn't holed out that 7-iron, and if you had three-putted only twelve times at the tournament, you might today be an assistant pro at Goat Hills."

What Do You Look At?

WHAT DO YOU look at when you look at the ball?
If I looked at the back of the ball, I would hook it.

If I looked at the top of the ball, a thin shot would be the result.

If I looked at the inside rear quarter of the ball, I would have too much to think about.

When I look at you, do I look at your eyes? Your nose? Your mouth? No, I am aware of these features, but what I see is the whole you.

And that's what I think you should see when you look at a golf ball. Be aware of the whole ball, but not intent on any one part of it.

Telephone Lesson

SANDRA PALMER PHONED our home and asked Helen to ask me to help her with her follow-through.

I could hardly see her follow-through over the long-distance line, and it was difficult for Sandra to try to describe it to Helen, who tried to describe it to me.

Finally I said, "The follow-through is a result of what has gone before it. Ask Sandra what her problem is with striking the ball."

Helen said, "She says she leaves too many shots out to the right."

I said, "Tell her to toe in her club a little before she places her hands on the grip."

This is the same thing as strengthening her grip, which I couldn't do unless I could see her hands on the club.

It's just an aspirin, not a cure. I felt like a doctor of a bygone era, when a person would call with an ailment and the doctor would say, "Take an aspirin and phone me tomorrow."

But I know that toeing-in the club would straighten her shot, and that would have to affect her follow-through.

A Future in Golf

ONE OF OUR members, George McCall, mentioned to me that a former Texas player, Martin Alday, had won the championship at Midland Country Club. George told me Martin's caddie was a sharp kid who probably had a good future in golf. George asked if we could find a summer job at our club for the kid, and would I give him some lessons instead of paying him a wage?

That is how I met Terry Jastrow.

Terry was about sixteen, a blond, good-looking boy, full of enthusiasm. I don't know what he expected when he showed up for work, but the first thing he got was a lecture.

"A lot of you Midland boys have daddies in the oil business, and you think you can get things handed to you right away," I said. "But golf at your level has nothing to do with money. I am going to start with you at the beginning, with your grip and stance, and if you become a good player it will be step by step, and it might be very slow."

I put Terry to work as a bag boy, loading and unloading and cleaning clubs for the members.

In his off hours, I sent Terry to the opposite end of the practice range at our club on Riverside Drive. He thought he was a fair player already, but his grip was too strong to travel outside west Texas. I told Terry he could hit nothing but 9-irons. I told him to think of clipping the grass with a weed cutter.

Now and then I would go visit Terry at the far end of the range to see how he was doing. I would touch his hands and pick at the calluses. Terry had the habit of "motorcycling," twisting his hands onto the grip rather than placing them there. This is the main cause for calluses.

About the time Terry would think I had forgotten him, I would show up again and watch him for a while. Eventually he graduated from a 9-iron to a 7-iron. It was several weeks before I let him hit a wood, and even then I took the driver out of his bag.

At the end of that first summer, Terry qualified for the championship flight of the state junior tournament and made it all the way to the finals before losing.

The next summer, Terry reported for work at Austin Country Club again. I set him to digging irrigation ditches.

He still had to practice at the far end of the range, but I let him play the course if it wasn't too crowded. He usually played with Tommy Kite and Barbara Puett.

That second summer, Terry won the state junior, beating John Mahaffey in the finals. Terry was medalist in the national junior and went to the quarterfinals before Lanny Wadkins knocked him out.

I thought Terry might enroll at the University of Texas, where his brother Kenny was already a student. But Terry's mind was set on being a golf pro, and the University of Houston had the dominant program in college golf at the time. Terry became a Houston Cougar.

Next thing I knew I saw a photo in *Sports Illustrated* of Terry being given a golf lesson by Houston coach Dave Williams. Williams was running a very successful program, but he didn't play golf or teach it, that I had ever heard of.

Terry showed up at Austin Country Club for lessons.

*Tom Kite, Harvey, and Tinsley Penick,
with the U.S. Open trophy.*

"I can't do it, Terry," I said. "I see that you are studying with Coach Williams, and I wouldn't want to tell you anything that might violate his teachings. One teacher at a time is plenty."

In his sophomore year, Terry went to work doing odd jobs for ABC-TV.

He told me, "I can't believe I will find a true source of happiness in needing to make five-foot putts week after week."

It turned out that Terry did indeed have a bright future in golf, but it was as a television producer and director rather than as a player.

And who do you think was producing the telecast when Tommy Kite won the U.S. Open at Pebble Beach?

Terry said, "When Tommy finally holed out, I was so full of joy that I took off my headset and went into an office by myself and wept for half an hour."

It took me that long just to get my toes uncurled.

Playing Hurt

ALTHOUGH IT LOOKS like such a peaceful game, golfers are beset with all sorts of injuries from muscle sprains to bad backs, from torn rotator cuffs to broken bones.

The one thing an injured golfer wants to know first is, "How can I keep playing?"

A friend sprained his left ankle on the second tee on the first day of a golfing trip to Scotland. He hobbled off the course in agony at the ninth and had a doctor tape the sprained ankle in a splint. He played for two weeks in Scotland on the sprained ankle, and by the time he came home, he had torn a ligament in his right knee because of it.

He told me he was playing at Royal Musselburgh, limping along as well as he could, when a woman appeared and called his caddie aside for a brief warning chat.

"What does she want?" my friend asked when the woman left.

The caddie said, "She wants you to get off the golf course."

"But why? There's no one pressing behind us."

The caddie said, "Aye, but she says sooner or later the gimp won't be able to keep up."

My friend told his caddie, "From now on, you find all my drives about 275 yards down the middle of the fairway." And he kept going.

If you have sore knees, they will be less painful if you wear rubber-sole shoes rather than spikes. In Scotland and England, where players walk, and walk fast, rubber-sole shoes are very popular.

A sore shoulder in the rotator cuff area is a common problem. You should ice it after you play. Exercise your shoulder often, swinging your arms in slow circles to keep your muscles from tightening.

Above all, you Seasoned Citizens especially, set aside a full five minutes to stretch before a round. If you don't have time both to stretch and hit practice balls, I suggest that you choose to stretch. Loosen up the grease, as Darrell Royal says. This will put you in shape to play much better than will rushing through a small bucket of balls.

The small bones of the hands are very susceptible to injuries, especially by good players who swing that club at upwards of 115 miles an hour.

Lee Trevino recently had surgery on his thumb. Ben

Crenshaw had a sore left thumb and asked if I had any suggestion what he should do about it. I said he could try taking his left thumb off the handle in his grip, the way the great Henry Picard did. That's why Picard started gripping the club in that fashion—because of a thumb injury.

Ben tried it for a few swings and was free of pain. But I am happy to say he promptly returned to his regular grip, which is a thing of beauty.

Many golfers get back injuries from bending over the wrong way to take the ball out of the cup. An orthopedist told me there would be far fewer back injuries if golfers would learn to sit down and cross one leg over the other to tie their shoes, instead of standing up straight and reaching down for the laces.

As golfers grow older they are subject to aches and pains of arthritis, bursitis, and other symptoms of aging. I know many who gulp down a handful of pain pills before they tee off.

Jack Nicklaus, Arnold Palmer, Tom Kite—the list goes on and on—have hurt their backs, but continue playing at the price of doing hours of exercises and stretching every day.

If you have just a minor, nagging injury that doesn't threaten to become a major one, there is one danger I can see if you keep on playing: A small hurt can take your mind off what it should be on—which is, taking dead aim.

The Feeling of Far

MANY TIMES OVER the years I have heard Byron Nelson say, "Just let it happen. Don't try to hit the ball far. Instead develop a feeling that the ball is going to go a long way without your really trying. And sure enough, it will."

My First Lesson

GROWING UP AS a caddie, I learned to play golf by trial and error and by copying the swings that I saw and liked.

The first lesson I ever had, I was already head pro at Austin Country Club.

My teacher was Walter Hagen.

We were playing an exhibition. I half-topped a couple of shots, and Hagen said, "Harvey, you want a word of advice?"

"Sure."

"You're trying too hard to keep your head down. Let your head be a little more free. Don't fall for this turn-in-a-barrel nonsense with your head fixed solidly in the center of your turn. You've got to move a little bit sideways along with your turn. This gets your weight onto your right foot and your head well behind the ball, so you can put power into your blow. It's like throwing a punch."

I took Hagen's advice, and I still teach that way.

Many times over the years I taught at PGA schools with great players like Paul Runyan, with whom I disagreed about the swing. Runyan was a turn-inside-a barrel player and teacher, but a notoriously short hitter. I felt Paul could have profited from a freer swing, as Hagen had taught me. However, Paul won two PGA championships and was elected to the Hall of Fame doing it his own way.

As I see it, all those PGA schools were like golf lessons for me. I especially liked listening to teachers who taught differently than I do. They made me think.

Also, I learned afresh each year when a new class of golfers came to our team at the university. Each of these youngsters had learned to play from someone—a pro, a friend, a relative, a caddie. In getting to know our new players, I learned whatever they had learned.

Some of the best tips I ever heard came from small-town club pros like Hardy Loudermilk from Jal, New Mexico. Hardy is the fellow who sent me a young pupil named Kathy Whitworth.

When people ask who my teacher was, I say, "Everybody."

But I always remember that first lesson from Walter Hagen.

Timing

ONE QUESTION I am usually asked at teaching seminars is, "What is timing, and is it different from rhythm and tempo?"

Timing is getting your muscles together to produce the maximum speed of the clubhead at impact and the angle of face square on the line to the target.

"Rhythm" and "tempo" are words I avoid. They are not the same as "timing."

There are plenty of good players who jump around during their swings, but meet the ball on the clubface at the right instant and get excellent results because of their timing.

The last player I wanted on my golf team was one who had to look good and have the prettiest swing without getting comparable results. Too often this player is satisfied with hitting stylish shots. Give me the player who is more concerned with putting the ball in the hole in the fewest strokes.

I know players who say they count in their heads—*one, two, three, four*—during the swing to help their rhythm or tempo. I don't see how they do it. If my mind is counting, how can I be taking dead aim?

Time to Move

I WAS WALKING through the airport in Atlanta when I encountered a friend, a famous golf pro from a famous club in Chicago.

"What are you doing here?" he asked.

"Teaching a seminar for the Georgia PGA," I said. "What are you doing here?"

"Changing planes. I'm going to Florida to look for a job."

I was surprised. "I thought you had one of the best jobs in the world."

He said, "I did, Harvey—until I agreed to serve on the handicap committee. I lowered a member's handicap by three strokes. The member caught me in the parking lot and said, 'Give me my three strokes back. I've had people killed for less than what you did, pro.'"

My friend packed a suitcase, and now he was on his way to Florida. I agreed that it was time to move.

The Downhill Lie

THE MOST FEARED fairway shot for the average golfer is the downhill lie.

A common mistake I see is that the player will try to stand up too straight.

The way to address the shot is with your body aligned on the same angle as the slope. For a right-handed player, this means your body will be slanted to the left.

Be sure to have enough weight on your left side to keep your balance.

Play the ball back in your stance. Swing the club with your hands and arms. Avoid the urge to raise up until your clubhead is through the ball.

Tension is a major wrecker of the shot off a downhill lie. Remember that your goal with this shot is not power, but a solid strike.

Haunted

MY CLOSE FRIEND Dick Metz, Wild Bill Mehlhorn, and I were paired at a tournament. Dick drew me aside as we were warming up.

He said, "I have to warn you, Harvey. Bill is so nervous

about his putting that he will insist on hitting first on every green to get it out of the way."

Bill Mehlhorn won twenty pro tournaments, played on the Ryder Cup team, and was a top teacher, but he was always haunted by the feeling that he was the worst putter in the world.

People ask me, "How is it possible for a person to win twenty pro tournaments and believe he is the worst putter in the world?" All I can answer is, "That's golf."

Dana X. Bible was the wildest hitter of the golf ball that I ever saw. He was a star player in football and baseball, and he won national championships as coach and athletic director at the University of Texas. But he couldn't shift his weight to his left side in his golf swing, no matter how many years of lessons I gave him. It seemed to be a total contradiction. This talented athlete could run for a touchdown or hit a home run, but to hit a golf shot he had to tee up the ball.

Of course, he didn't try to hide it. If you were playing with him for the first time, he would say, "I am going to tee up the ball whenever I want to, and you may feel free to do the same."

Our fairways in those days were scattered with worm casts, which D.X. used as tees when convenient. He insisted upon hitting up on the ball. Changing him was beyond my power.

I think people inherit quirky characteristics that may never show up except on a golf course.

In Bill Mehlhorn's case it was the contradiction of a superior golfer's being totally terrified of putting.

Hogan Whiffs It

IT WAS A CHARITY match. Morris Williams, Jr., and Ed Hopkins were teamed against Ben Hogan and me.

With a large gallery around the first tee and people lining the fairway, we were waiting for Hogan. At last here he came, staggering a bit, a crooked grin on his face, his cap slightly aslant.

I could hear gasps from the crowd. "What's wrong with Hogan?" people whispered. "Why, it looks like he's drunk!"

Hogan fell to his knees trying to put his ball on the tee. He struggled to his feet, squinted down the fairway, rubbed his eyes, lurched backwards. Murmurs from the gallery grew louder.

Ben took a mighty swipe at his drive and missed it.

He grunted. He waggled and knocked his ball backwards off the tee. A caddie replaced it. Hogan tried again and topped his drive about fifty yards.

Morris, Ed, and I hit decent drives. We marched down to Hogan's ball. Wobbling, Ben lashed at his ball and hit a big slice. His cap fell off. The caddie picked it up for him, and Hogan put his cap on sideways.

Finally we reached the green. Ben knocked his first putt some twenty feet past the hole. He was still away. His second putt again went twenty feet past the hole. The gallery was aghast. Staggering, Ben lined up his third putt—and somehow the ball dropped into the cup.

Retrieving the ball, Ben fell down again. I could see the dismay on the faces of the gallery.

Ben stood up, looked around at the people ringing the

green, and broke into a big smile. He straightened his cap. He said to me, "Okay, pardner, it's up to you on this hole. I'll do better from now on."

Suddenly the gallery caught on. Everybody started laughing.

Hogan wasn't drunk. He was just putting on a clown act for the people. Bob Hope couldn't have done it better.

It's hard to believe for golf fans who have grown up watching the great Ben Hogan, stern and impassive, winning major championships, but when he was younger Hogan was a terrific entertainer and salesman with a wonderful sense of humor.

The rest of the way, Ben played that charity match as if it were the U.S. Open. The college boys beat us 1-up.

Few people remembered the result of the match, but everyone that day remembered Hogan on the first hole. They talked about it for years. It was a side of Ben that not many galleries ever had a chance to see.

Where Is He?

I WAS ALWAYS SO quiet that Jimmy Demaret told me I ought to wear some of his brightly colored outfits just so people would know I was around.

I liked the way Ben Hogan and Walter Hagen dressed—gray and black and brown and white.

Game of Honor

GOLF IS A GAME of honor. If you are playing any other way, you are not getting the fullest satisfaction from it.

Observing the customs of honor should be so deeply ingrained that it never occurs to you to play dishonorably.

There have been countless examples of players calling penalty shots on themselves for violations that no one else saw—and in some cases losing tournaments because of it.

During the third round of the Kemper Open in 1993, Tommy Kite was leading and was paired with Grant Waite of New Zealand.

Near the fourth green, Waite took a drop from a Ground Under Repair area. As Waite prepared to hit to the green, Tommy looked over and noticed Waite's heel was still inside the Ground Under Repair marker.

This was a tournament Tommy wanted very much to win. It was his first strong showing since a back injury in the spring. It would have been so easy to glance away and pretend he hadn't seen where Waite was standing.

That is, it would have been easy for some people. For Tommy Kite, it was not even a consideration.

"We don't need any penalties here," Tommy said, pointing out the location of the New Zealander's heel.

If Waite had hit that shot, it would have been a two-stroke penalty. The penalty would have put Tommy in the lead by three. But, as I said, Tommy never gave it a thought.

Tommy said, "It would be pretty chicken for me to stand by and watch a guy accidentally break a rule and then say, 'By the way, add two strokes.' That's not golf. That's other sports where guys are trying to get every advantage they can."

Waite won the tournament by one shot. Tommy finished second.

I think I'm more proud of Tommy for that tournament than I am for his U.S. Open victory. An Open champion is a winner on the golf course. A person of honor is a winner everywhere.

PART III

---

from
*For All Who
Love the Game*

Lessons in the Afternoon

IT WAS EARLY on a hot Saturday afternoon in July. I had already been at the club watching Sandra Palmer hit balls for an hour or so. Now I was back at home in my lounge chair in the living room, feeling sort of achy and drained by the sun.

I thought I would have a bowl of soup and a sandwich for lunch. Then I would read my mail and answer a few letters before the Women's Open appeared on TV in a little while. Sandra was spending the weekend at our house, and she planned to come from the practice range to watch the tournament with me. Watching the Open while sitting with an Open champion like Sandra is a thrill for me. I knew it would pick up my spirits.

But my son, Tinsley, walked in the front door and said, "Dad, we need you at the club."

"What's the matter?" I asked.

"A woman needs your help."

"Does it have to be right now?" I asked.

"Dad, she has come a long way and is eager to see you."

Ordinarily what Tinsley had said would have roused me to get into my golf cart and return to the club at once. I could never turn down a woman in distress. On this day, though, with the temperature above one hundred degrees and several things at home I wanted to be doing, it was hard for me to think about moving.

"What seems to be her problem?" I asked.

"She can't get the ball into the air," Tinsley said.

That was all I needed to hear.

"Help me out of this chair," I said.

Teaching frustrated women golfers to hit the ball into the air is a challenge I love, one that when accomplished brings forth such a roar of joy from both the pupil and the teacher that I get goose bumps that make me feel I'm in the middle of an electrical storm.

An attractive woman was waiting in the practice area when I arrived in my golf cart. She introduced herself as Susan Baker. She said her husband, Jim, was out on the course playing golf. They lived back and forth between Houston and Washington, D.C., she said, but were in Austin to attend a wedding.

"Use your 7-iron and let me see you hit a few balls," I said.

What I needed to know first was whether her frustration was caused by the path of her swing or by the angle of her clubface.

Her swing looked pretty good to me, but every ball she hit rolled about thirty yards along the ground.

"I've had a number of lessons, and yet I just keep on doing this," she said.

I looked at her hands on the club. Her grip seemed reasonable. But having seen that her swing was all right, I knew her grip had to be the villain.

I asked her to remove her glove and take her grip again.

Sure enough, that is where the culprit lay concealed.

When she took her grip, both hands were pretty much under the handle. But then she twisted her flesh around so that her bad grip was disguised to look like a reasonable grip.

"Would you mind if we back up a little and start over?" I asked.

"Please do," she said.

"Let's forget the word 'grip.' Let's just think about placing your hands on the club. Please let me guide you into placing them. Look at how your hands hang naturally at your sides. Now place your left hand on the handle with a natural feeling so that you can glance down and see three knuckles. That's right. That's how I want it. Leave it just like that, without twisting. Now place your right hand on the handle so that your lifeline in your palm fits against your thumb. That's very good."

I leaned over and touched her left elbow.

"Let go of the tension in your elbows," I said.

Instead, she let go of the club with her hands. That always happens at first. I asked her to place her hands back on the handle as she had done before, without rolling her left arm or twisting her flesh. Just place her hands on the handle and hold it lightly.

I touched her left elbow again.

"Without letting go of the club, allow the tension to go out of your elbows and your shoulders," I said.

I saw her elbows soften. Her shoulders became less rigid.

I clapped my hands with approval.

"Now look at a spot on the grass and make me a nice practice swing, hitting the spot."

Susan made several good-looking practice swings that brushed the grass.

"Now put a tee in the ground," I said. "We don't need a ball yet. Just a tee. Please make me a nice swing and hit that tee. Feel that you are swinging easy, but hit that tee hard enough to cut it off or knock it out of the ground."

After Susan did this half a dozen times, clipping that tee with a good, smooth, full swing, I asked her to put a ball on the tee.

"Now, disregard the ball but go ahead and give that tee a healthy crack," I said.

Susan hit that ball out of my sight. My eyes are not as

sharp as they once were, but I could tell she had hit it well over a hundred yards in the air with her 7-iron.

Susan screamed with pleasure. She jumped up and down. She leaped over and kissed me. I was tingling from head to toe.

"I never thought it was possible!" she said. "Let's do it again."

She did it several more times, cutting off the tee with a nice swing, the ball flying out there more than a hundred yards, plenty high with a little tail on it.

"Now, pull out your 3-wood," I said.

I saw a moment of fear in her eyes.

"Trust me," I said. "You know how to do it. Treat this club just as you have been treating the other one."

Well, what do you think happened?

With her 3-wood, Susan hit the ball 170 yards.

She was astonished. She was so thrilled that tears rushed to her eyes.

My arms turned white with goose bumps.

"Now, please listen to me," I said. "I want you to remember. What we did here today—or rather what you did—it works the same in Houston or in Washington, D.C., as it does at Austin Country Club. Always remember that, and you will be fine from now on."

I asked Susan to enjoy the game of golf to its fullest and please come back and see me anytime she thought she needed me.

"Please give my regards to your husband," I said.

Driving me home in my golf cart, Tinsley said, "Do you know who her husband is?"

"Jim," I said.

"Her husband is James Baker. He was secretary of state and chief of staff for President Bush."

I am not a political person, but I do have a soft spot for President Bush. He wrote me a letter about golf and life that he hand typed himself. His letter is framed on the wall of my little bedroom at the front of the house. In the middle of the night when pain keeps me awake, I often look at that letter and pinch myself to be sure it's real, that a president sat down and typed a letter to a grown caddie.

Back at the house, Sandra was watching the Open on television. As I settled into my lounge chair again, Sandra caught me up on what had been happening.

The Swedish star Helen Alfredsson had started the Saturday round with a big lead on the field. But her game was faltering.

As I began watching, she was in the struggle of losing eight strokes to par in ten holes. It was painful to see. I felt sorry for her. Such things happen to even the best players, and all golfers know it. But still my heart went out to this handsome young woman who has so much talent.

All of a sudden, with several holes yet to play, the television network cut short my suffering on Helen Alfredsson's behalf, as well as what joy I would be receiving from the rise of Patty Sheehan and other fine players in the Women's Open—and my pleasure at listening to the TV commentary by Judy Rankin, who used to be a pupil of mine.

A man's voice on the television told us they were leaving the Women's Open because their time was up. The network switched to some kind of track meet in Russia.

"Do you think they would do that if this was the Men's Open?" Sandra said. "What if some prominent man player was losing a big lead, and some other prominent men players were making a charge? Would the network switch away to a track meet that was taped earlier in another country? Would they dare do that to men?"

"I don't think so," I said.

"You know darn well they wouldn't," Sandra said.

She headed toward the door.

"I'm going back to the practice tee," she said. "They

Harvey with Sandra Palmer, 1964.

won't let me watch the Women's Open, but they can't stop me from practicing."

So I read my mail and answered letters. It was too hot for anything else. But I felt better now than when I came home earlier in the day.

Remembering Susan Baker's cry of pleasure when she saw that ball fly out there 170 yards, I kept smiling. Moments like that make my life fulfilled.

And if enough Susan Bakers find joy and satisfaction in the great game of golf, maybe someday that network will treat the world's finest women players with the same respect it reserves for men.

A Practice Procedure

NEARLY EVERY DAY, I see golfers out there banging away at bucket after bucket of balls, and if I were to ask them what they were doing, they would say, "Why, what does it look like I'm doing, Harvey? I'm practicing."

They are all getting exercise, all right. But few of them are really practicing.

If you stand there and hit balls without purpose long enough, you might start doing it right and eventually find out how to do it wrong.

Let me suggest a practice procedure that I know gets results.

After you have done your stretching, which you should always take time to do, pull out your wedge and hit five full shots with it. Then put it away.

Now use your 7-iron. Hit five shots with it. No matter how good they are, resist the urge to hit more in an effort to "groove it." Chances are you might lose it.

Put your 7-iron aside and take out your 3-wood. Hit five shots with your 3-wood, always aiming at a target. Then put it away.

Now pick up your 7-iron again and hit five more shots with it. Then put it away.

If you feel like it, you may now pull out your driver and hit three or four balls with it. Try your best to hit them good, as though you were on the first tee. But if they are not great drives, forget it. Put your driver away.

You have now hit a few more than twenty full shots.

That's enough full shots for an efficient practice session.

Now take your putter, wedge, and a couple of chipping clubs and go spend the rest of your practice time sharpening your short game. This is where you are going to lower your scores.

The Card Table— Under and Under

USUALLY I USE a bench for this instruction, but a card table will do just as well.

As an aid to practicing your chip shots, picture in your mind that there is a card table a few feet beyond your swing.

If you can practice with a real card table—or a real bench—so much the better.

Hit your chip shot so that you feel you are going to hit

the ball under the bench or card table. You want the ball to be on the ground quickly and rolling in a chip shot.

A Fundamental

YOUR HANDS MUST lead your clubhead into contact with the ball on every swing, from the putter through the driver.

On putts and chips, your hands must lead or stay even with the clubhead all the way through the finish of the stroke.

There are as many variations to the swing as there are to individual styles of walking. But in a good swing, this one thing never varies: Your hands lead your clubhead through the downswing.

There was a fellow at River Oaks in Houston who wrote a book about his belief not only that the hands lead the clubhead but that, furthermore, the wrists must never consciously uncock.

The first week Jackson Bradley showed up for work as head pro at River Oaks, this fellow cornered him and said, "Let's get it straight right from the beginning. I know more about the golf swing than you will ever know."

Jackson is a great teacher and doesn't need me to defend him against anyone.

But we all must admit the fellow at River Oaks was onto one solid fundamental of the golf swing that every good teacher and good player agree on:

Your hands always lead your clubhead into contact with the ball on every stroke.

On putts and chips, your hands must lead or stay even with the clubface all the way through. This is a very important thing to remember.

What's Your Hurry?

THERE MAY SOMEWHERE be a good golfer whose backswing is too slow, but that person has not set foot on any golf course I know of in the last ninety years.

There's an old joke that golf hustlers are always on the watch for a player with a fat wallet and a fast backswing.

Bobby Jones said two of the best pieces of advice he ever received from teacher Stewart Maiden are "You don't hit it with your backswing" and "Hit it hard, it'll come down someplace."

I love a slow, smooth takeaway and backswing.

A slow backswing gives you time to make a good turn and stay balanced as you are gathering yourself for the forward blow.

I am not in favor of the pause at the top, which is the only disagreement I have with Tommy Armour. I think a swing must be a swing, and if it comes to a stop partway, it is not a swing.

Of course there is the moment of transition from backward to forward, but the most important part of this is automatically taken care of when you plant your left heel on the ground and your weight shifts to the left.

When you plant that left heel and at the same moment, in a single move, bring your right elbow back to your side—

Harvey posts the club rules;
Helen is at far right.

the Magic Move—the transition takes place without your needing to think about it.

You store up energy going back and release that energy coming forward. Like throwing a punch. Like throwing a baseball. Like serving at tennis.

Some of the top players are fast swingers, backwards and forwards in a blur. This is natural for them. If I tried to make Ben Hogan or Tom Watson or Lanny Wadkins take the club back slowly, I would be crazy.

But in nearly every session I have with Tom Kite and Sandra Palmer, to name two great players who tend to let their backswings get a little too fast for their golfing personalities, I urge them to slow down in the takeaway.

Both Sandra and Tommy always look surprised when I say they have gotten fast. But after they put their minds to it for a few swings, they see the results.

A Golf Tip

As a teacher who is well acquainted with the frailties of the golfing mind, I laughed out loud at what writer Stephen Potter said about golf tips.

He said he was eager for the golfing magazines to appear in his mail each month so that he could clip out the latest golf tips.

"I show them to my opponents," he said.

I know a fellow in Austin, Doug Holloway, who was a high handicapper until about ten years ago, when he went through the golf school that Chuck Cook used to teach at the Hills of Lakeway.

This fellow spent three long days hitting hundreds of balls with Chuck, and within a month was shooting in the 70s. Often a pupil will rapidly improve for a while and then suddenly go backwards, forgetting everything that was taught. But not this fellow, Holloway. Ten years later he is still scoring regularly in the middle 70s.

His secret is that he made notes of everything Chuck taught him and devoutly follows those same teachings to this day. When something goes awry with his game, he goes back to the notes he took from Chuck. This always straightens him out, because he knows for a fact that this teaching works for him.

He has never read a golf tip in a magazine or a golf instructional book since those three days with Chuck. He just keeps doing the same thing, and it keeps working.

Golf tips can be wonderful, but they can also hurt your game. If an opponent gives you a tip, ignore it.

Preferably with the help of a teacher, once you have found a swing that works for you, stick with it. If it falters, re-examine the basic things that you were doing when you were playing well.

You may find the problem is that a golf tip has gotten into the machinery somewhere and changed your swing for the worse.

The Vital Long Chip Shot

IF YOU ARE new to the game, you are constantly faced with long chip shots—your ball a yard or so off the green, the pin maybe fifty feet away.

You must learn this shot. It is vital if you hope to lower your scores. As you become a better player, you will still find yourself hitting long chip shots from the fringe. Not as often as when you were a beginner, but you will miss greens and need a good long chip shot to make yourself a par.

One big difference between a scratch player and one with a 15 handicap is that the scratch player will usually chip the ball within two or three feet of the cup and walk away with a par. The higher handicapper will chip to six or eight feet, miss the putt, perhaps miss the next putt, and walk away with a bogey or a double.

As I repeat daily, a golfer who can chip and putt is a match for anybody. A golfer who cannot is a match for nobody.

Learning the chip shot is the best way to start learning the game.

Chipping is not like putting.

Many players, including some good ones, use their putting grips and putting strokes on a long chip shot, which is fine with me as long as they also happen to be using their putter from off the green.

I prefer that you stay with a strong grip, the V's to the right shoulder. Remember that chipping is a little drive, and a drive is a big chip shot.

Many high handicappers want to use a wedge from the edge of the green and try to lob the ball up to the hole, but they do not have the skill for this shot.

On a chip shot, play the ball in about the middle of your stance. Put slightly more weight on your left foot. Many use an open stance, but I don't think it is good for everyone. My own preference is for a square stance.

Grip down on the handle, but stop just short of touching the shaft. People will say to you, "Choke down on it." "Choke" is a word you want to dismiss from your mind.

The backswing and the forward swing should be the

same length, as would happen if you were throwing a ball underhanded. A long follow-through tends to come with deceleration, but what you want is acceleration

Clip the grass with the clubhead when you swing.

Make a couple of practice strokes. This is a shot when you should feel the distance to the hole in your hands and fingers.

Select the chipping club with the flattest blade that will get your ball onto the green and rolling the soonest. A 7-iron is a good all-around chipping club, but there are shots, especially the vital long chips, when you may want a 5-iron or lower.

Remember the fundamental that, in the chip shot, the hands not only must lead the clubhead into contact with the ball; the hands must also stay ahead of—at least even with—the clubhead on the follow-through.

When you practice this shot, chip from different distances. You are nearly always close to the line on a chip; it is the distance you must develop the touch for.

Practice builds confidence, and with confidence you can start getting down in two on those long chip shots.

When you can turn three into two regularly, you will be a sought-after partner.

A Matter of Touch

IN MY EARLY years as the pro at Austin Country Club, we used to keep about sixty sets of golf clubs in racks against the wall.

They were clubs that belonged to members.

On rainy days we would sometimes play a little game. For a bet of a dime, I would shut my eyes and someone would pick up a club from a bag and put the club into my hands.

With my eyes closed I would rub my fingers over the clubhead and the shaft and feel the wrapped grip, and I would sink into my memory, and in a few moments I would say, "Why, this is Dr. Miller's mashie." Or, "Yes, this is Mrs. Armstrong's niblick."

I was nearly always right.

There was no trickery to it. Many of those clubs I had held with my own hands. I would shave the wooden shafts down with a piece of glass to get them to the flexibility my member needed. The clubs I hadn't made, I learned well anyway, because it was my responsibility to keep the clubs cleaned and in good repair, so they were often in my hands. Each of these clubs was made for a specific person.

Then along came steel shafts, and manufacturers were able to mass-produce sets of clubs for sale in pro shops and sporting goods stores.

Now it is all the rage once again to have your golf clubs custom made. Rather than just grabbing a set off the shelf, more golfers are being measured for height and length of arm and swing speed, and are buying clubs that are supposed to fit them.

Tour players are constantly fiddling with their clubs, changing shafts, bending the angles, adding or subtracting weight.

Any tour player could walk down the line at a practice range and hit good-looking shots with a wide assortment of clubs chosen from each bag, but only the tour player knows how satisfactory the shots really are. The high handicapper gets more obvious benefit from custom fitting than does the pro, but it's the pro whose clubs always fit.

A rapidly growing number of golfers buy the component parts—shafts, clubheads, and grips—from supply houses or from catalogs and put their clubs together themselves or hire someone to do the assembling. Partly this is a reaction to rising costs; a top line of famous irons today can cost more than a new car did when I was young. Partly it is because custom-made clubs make good sense and are easily available.

I think, also, it is because to put together a golf club with your own hands is a satisfying thing. It is something you never forget.

Steady Head

I AM VERY careful when discussing the position of the head in the golf swing, because it is so easy to be misunderstood.

When I say it is all right for the head to move a little bit backward during the swing, so long as the head never moves forward until after the ball is gone, some pupils hear only the words "all right for the head to move."

In no time they are bobbing up and down like turkeys or turning their chins backward and forward as their shoulders turn, and they lunge and swoop and try to locate the ball their swing is supposed to hit.

It is true that all the good players I have ever seen move their heads during their swings, always backwards. Most good players move their heads even farther backwards an inch or so as the forward swing passes the chin.

The good player's head always stays behind the ball.

Having heard these teachings, a pupil will sometimes nod and remember only, "It's all right for my head to move."

If you put it that way, then, no, it is wrong for your head to move.

You should think about keeping a steady head.

Your head will move anyway, though you probably won't even feel it. But the mental picture of keeping a steady head may be the thought you need if your shots are erratic.

Louise Suggs teaches that the most important feature of the swing is the position of the head. She thinks of her head as the hub on a wagon wheel and her arms as the spokes as the wagon wheel rolls around the hub. If your head, the hub, jerks or tilts or bobs up and down, your spokes will break down or the wheel will come off.

Many fine teachers adopt that same image—to think of your head as the hub around which the swing revolves, and thus to understand that it must be held steady.

I have heard Jack Nicklaus say that his first teacher, Jack Grout, taught him as a youngster to play with a steady head by grasping Jack's hair and holding it during the swing. Grout regarded keeping the head still as a universal, unarguable fundamental in golf.

Bobby Jones said that in his experience the correct swing was performed beneath a head that is "practically stationary." Jones said it is a sound concept to think of the head as the anchor of the swing.

To some pupils, then, I ask that they think of keeping a steady head.

This is totally different advice from "keep your head down." You keep your head somewhat up, and you keep it steady as your swing goes around beneath it.

When I say steady head, I do not mean petrified. I would use the word "practically," as Jones does, were it not that some would take this qualifier as license to move the head forward.

Moving your head forward during a golf swing before the ball is gone is one of the very worst things you can do.

The thought of keeping a steady head is a swing picture that does wonders for many pupils.

Be Yourself

KATHY WHITWORTH WAS in a slump that made her feel so miserable and frustrated that she left the tour and drove to Austin to see me.

I had been her teacher since Hardy Loudermilk sent her to me as a teenager from New Mexico.

It was obvious in our first few minutes on the practice tee that, since the last time I had seen her, Kathy had shortened her swing so much that she had almost no backswing.

Why would a great player like Kathy have changed her swing? It happens because golfers—even the best of them—are so sensitive to suggestion. Most golfers, in fact, are downright gullible and will listen to advice from almost anyone.

What had happened to Kathy was that when her slump began, other players and teachers started approaching her on the practice tee and offering "cures."

Someone had planted in Kathy's mind that her trouble was caused by picking up the club on the takeaway. She was told to push the club back. Kathy concentrated on pushing the club back, and her swing became short and artificial, and pretty soon her wonderful golf game went awry.

"I'm desperate, Harvey," she told me. "I'm not hitting the ball well enough to beat anybody. What am I doing wrong?"

I avoid talking to pupils about what they are doing wrong. I talk about what they are doing right. I could easily

Harvey with Kathy Whitworth.

have told Kathy that her backswing was too short, but that would have solved nothing. What I needed to discover was why her backswing had become too short. By digging to the cause of the problem, I could fix it with a good dose of medicine that would really make her well instead of just treating the symptoms.

But after three days of watching Kathy hit balls, I hadn't helped her a bit.

It was painful for both of us when she climbed into her car and drove away from Austin to return to the tour.

The night she left, I lay awake thinking about her. When eventually I slept, I dreamed about her.

In the morning while I was shaving, the answer popped into my mind.

I phoned the next tournament and left word for Kathy to call me.

When I heard her anxious voice on the line, I said, "Kathy, when you first came to me as a youngster, you had a natural cock of the wrists at the start of your backswing. That's what is missing from your swing now. You are not being yourself. Go back to cocking that club off at the beginning like you used to."

"You never mentioned a natural early wrist cock to me before," she said.

I never mentioned her footwork or her shoulder turn, either, because there was no need. She did those things well in her own style the first time I ever saw her.

"Forget all those things other people are telling you, and just play golf the way you know how," I said. "You are the one and only Kathy Whitworth. So play golf the way Kathy Whitworth plays."

Kathy won three of the next four tournaments on the tour, simply by returning to being true to herself.

Remain true to what your own inner knowledge says, despite conflicting advice, even if it is well meant. No matter how big you get, always remember it was your fundamentals and your own swing that got you there.

Sandra Palmer phoned me from a tournament after a shaky round. I had heard Sandra had been listening to practice tee advice and was losing the naturalness of her swing.

I told her, "Your muscles are smarter than you think they are. Your muscles will think for themselves if you will let them remember the swing that made you the tour's leading money winner."

The golf swing is largely a matter of trust.

My Banquet Speech

MORE THAN TWENTY years ago I was chosen Teacher of the Year by the Metropolitan Golf Association and was invited to a big, fancy banquet at the Waldorf in New York to accept my award.

I worried for days about my acceptance speech. I wrote it and rewrote it and then rewrote it again. Helen was amused by my labors.

Flying to New York City, we were on the same plane with Texas governor Alan Shivers, a friend and pupil. Helen told him that I must be going to make a powerful speech, considering all the effort I had put into it.

The night of the banquet, Claude Harmon was the first speaker. Claude could get pretty wound up, and he talked for quite a while. Following Claude to the podium came Howard Cosell. Howard had remarks for everyone at the head table and for many in the audience, and this was before he even got into the meat of his speech.

By the time I was called up to the microphone, wearing my white dinner jacket, we had been in that room for hours. I looked out at the crowd and all I said was, "This is mighty humbling. Thank you."

I sat down to cheers and applause from a weary, grateful audience. Sometimes knowing when to shut up is the best thing a teacher can do.

An Outlook on Putting

To SINK A CRUCIAL long putt with the tournament on the line, I would select Kathy Whitworth to do the job more often than any other player I have ever seen, and I include the names of Smith, Cotton, Jones, and Crenshaw in my thinking.

Kathy has the outlook on the putting stroke that it is just a smaller version of the full swing and that putting is just another part of the game.

Many players hate putting. It drives them crazy. The very idea of a little putt counting for at least as much as, and probably more than, a lusty drive from the tee is too much to bear.

I know a lot of people would be happy with a game that counted for score the number of fairways and greens hit, and closest to the pin, and entirely left out putting.

But Kathy regards putting as a continuation of what starts with her on the first tee. If she is swinging well, she knows she will putt well.

Kathy practices putting less than any other great player ever did, I would guess. To her, putting is all feel, and if her golfing senses tell her that her swing and her outlook are good, then she avoids the practice green.

However, Kathy is a believer in putting on the carpet to keep her stroke smooth. We have spent many hours stroking putts on the carpet at the Penick home.

To Kathy the most important thing in putting is to stay steady over the ball. If she misses a putt, she says it is usually because her head has moved, or her eyes may have flicked back and forth with the putter head.

When Kathy was playing at her peak, she said she would get a mental picture of the line of the putt, and her hands would feel the distance and control the stroke, and putting was as simple as pointing her finger.

I always taught letting your putt die at the hole. The never-up-never-in school leads, I believe, to three-putts. By firmly rapping your putts two or three feet past the hole, you put too much strain on your nerves trying to make them coming back.

Betsy Rawls, another great putter, probably three-putted less than any champion. Betsy's putting philosophy was to hit her ball to the hole. As a Phi Beta Kappa in physics, Betsy understood mentally as well as sensuously that if she kept hitting her putts to the hole at the right speed, a good number of them would drop.

Kathy sees putting the same way as Betsy. She strokes her putts to the cup and no farther, knowing the ones that hit the lip will be moving gently enough to fall in.

Her putter is a Walter Hagen Tomboy that Wilson sent her in the early '60s. It's dented and nicked by time, the shaft glued back together after she whacked the ground with it once in frustration.

When I see a pupil constantly changing putters, as if that will automatically help the putting, I like to tell them about Kathy's old Tomboy putter.

With that putter, she won eighty-eight professional tour tournaments, the most of any woman or man in the history of the game.

Mickey Wright has an old cash-in putter with lead tape on the toe and more lead stuck to the heel. Mickey won eighty-two professional tour tournaments with that putter, and she still uses it today.

To me this proves that once you find a putter you like, stay with it through bad times as well as good. If the putts stop dropping for a while, the fault lies in your thinking and your stroke, not in your faithful old putter.

Kathy told me she refused to think of making or missing any putt. In more than twenty years on the tour, she always kept the consequences of every putt out of her mind. Instead, she thought of making a good stroke.

Refresh Yourself

THE BEST THING to drink on the golf course is water, and lots of it.

If your course is lacking in watering holes, bring a gallon jug from home. On a hot summer day, you get dehydrated in a hurry, even if you can't tell it. Remind yourself to take a few swigs of water every couple of holes.

Avoid those soft drinks that are loaded with sugar. A sugar drink may give you a burst of energy, but it will last a very short while and leave you feeling weaker than before.

The same is true of a candy bar.

Many players on the LPGA tour—like Pat Bradley,

Nancy Lopez, and Patty Sheehan—carry with them apples, bananas, sandwiches, and packages of dried fruit. These will keep your energy and your blood sugar up. The new sports health bars that look like candy are advertised to do the same thing, but I never tried one of them.

For years it was popular for golfers to stop at the clubhouse for lunch at the turn. I'm sure this revived some players—and put others to sleep—but there is no way this long, stomach-filling pause could have helped their scores.

The Basic Shot

LEARN ONE BASIC shot that you can hit under pressure and stick with it. If you have a good basic shot, you will rarely ever have to hit a fancy one.

Learning

IT IS EASIER to learn something new than it is to unlearn something that you have been doing wrong for a long time.

This is why it is so important to get started in golf with the proper teaching.

For example, if you have been slicing the ball ever since you began playing the game, and you come to me and ask

From a tribute to Harvey: (clockwise from top left)
Betsy Rawls, Peggy Wilson, Betsy Cullen, Judy Kimball,
Mickey Wright, and Kathy Whitworth.

me to unlearn the slice for you, what I usually do is teach you how to hook the ball instead.

If you had gone to a teacher in the beginning, you would not have developed that slice. Playing golf with a slice prevents you from enjoying the full experience of the game. But the slice is the common shot of the beginner and the occasional player. The anguish of a constant slice drives many newcomers away from the game.

Rather than giving up on what could become a grand, long-lasting experience, turn both hands until your V's point at your right shoulder and learn that Magic Move—bring your right arm to your right ribs on your downswing at the same time you plant your weight on your left heel.

It is easier to teach a beginner to hit a little tail hook than it is to teach the same shot to a player with an ingrained slice.

If you will learn the correct fundamentals at the start, your progress in golf will be much faster and also much more fun.

The Left Wrist

PROBABLY THE MOST common fault among high-handicap players is the breaking down of the left wrist. This is also the most difficult fault to cure.

On a full swing, your left forearm or your whole left arm must rotate through the shot. High handicappers usually slap at the ball and flap their left wrists.

You must learn to keep your hands ahead of—or at least even with—the clubhead until the ball is gone.

The first teacher who finds an easy, quick way to cure the left wrist breakdown will become a wealthy person with students waiting in line from here to Hong Kong.

Women's Grips

ALMOST EVERY WOMAN who comes to me is guided into a stronger grip first thing.

I want the left hand particularly strong, with three knuckles showing when you glance down. Make it this strong by moving your hand over, not by rolling your arm inward. Beware that you do not roll your arm. Keep it at ease instead.

With the right hand, I am not quite so insistent. I like the right hand V to point toward the right shoulder, but we may take the privilege of moving the right hand into a weaker position if we are curing a hook.

Everyone who knows me knows what a stickler I am about the grip. As I say, if you have a bad grip, you don't want a good swing.

The interlocking grip is proper for most women because of their small hands. Many of the stronger women players prefer the overlapping grip because of larger or more muscular hands. Sometimes I will urge a woman pupil to abandon her interlocking grip and change to the overlapping if it is a move I think will help her natural swing.

After eighty years of observing women's hands on golf clubs, beginning as a caddie, I believe that just recently I have decided I would change my teaching to women if I could go back to the beginning.

I would put nearly all my women pupils in the so-called ten-finger grip.

I believe now that placing all eight fingers and two thumbs on the handle presents a woman with more power and control.

Some of my pupils, like Cindy Figg-Currier and Alice Ritzman, added yards they needed once we changed their grips to the full-finger. I coaxed Sandra Palmer to try the full-finger grip for more distance. She agreed it seemed to give her power and solid contact, but Sandra didn't trust the grip enough to use it in a tournament.

As I lie in my bed at night and think of past lessons, I find myself wishing I had urged the full-finger grip on many more of my women pupils. I now believe it is the best and most natural grip for a woman to use.

Post It

NOTHING MOVES FASTER than a good thought disappearing from the mind of a golfer.

Our fine University of Texas champion Justin Leonard, winner of the U.S. Amateur and the NCAA individual among other titles, turned pro and won a lot of money in his first few weeks on the tour.

Then Justin lost confidence in his swing and missed the cut six tournaments in a row.

He went home to Dallas to see his longtime teacher Randy Smith at Royal Oaks. They spent five hours together on the practice tee, not trying to improve Justin's swing but to put it back the way it used to be before he began traveling and competing with the professionals.

As his good old successful thoughts came back, Justin wrote them down on a card. He and his teacher decided on seven good fundamental things for Justin to remember, beginning with his grip.

Justin wrote down seven good thoughts on a card and fastened the card to his yardage book, where he would see them as often as needed.

So you see, you high handicappers are not alone in forgetting the good thoughts you learn at lessons or while making your way around the golf course.

But I doubt if more than a few of you have bothered to write down those good thoughts as you learned them. If you did write them down and kept them within reach, you would improve your handicap and your confidence.

Universal Advice

I ASKED MARY LENA FAULK if, after her long career as a top player and teacher, she could decide on any one piece of advice she would give to all golfers, regardless of sex, physique, age, or ability.

"Yes, I certainly can," she said. "I would tell all golfers to remember the game is played one stroke at a time. Hit the ball that's in front of you, and do your best on every shot. You can't play the next shot until after you have played this one.

"I don't care who you are, you're not going to hit it perfect every time. Do your best with what you've got today, and do it one shot at a time. That's what I would tell every golfer."

When to Offer Golf Advice to Your Spouse

IF HE ASKS.

Perceptions

BEN HOGAN SAID when he was hitting the ball at his very purest, his golf clubs felt "little tiny."

He said his clubs felt so light that he was hardly aware of them. And yet, Ben used a very heavy driver with the stiffest shaft I ever saw. I doubt I could even have swung his driver, but to Hogan it was like a feather when he was at the top of his game.

Helen, 1946.

Another Reason to Clip the Tee

MANY HIGH HANDICAPPERS flinch at the moment of impact. They actually slow down, even seem to draw back, and they rear their bodies upright as if trying to escape the confrontation of club and ball.

The simplest way to cure this fault is to clip the tee.

If you make a full free swing and concentrate on knocking the tee out from under the ball, it's impossible for your body to lift up.

I get many letters from pupils and friends who want to know how they can ever give up the crutch of clipping the tee and go to the reality of playing the ball as it lies.

My suggestion is that as you practice clipping the tee with your irons, you gradually lower the tee until it is level with the earth. Just knowing the tee is there will give you confidence. Once you have confidence, you can take it to the course and not need a tee.

But when problems come up, go to the practice range and resume clipping the tee. This will usually set your swing right.

Exercise

PEOPLE WHO SAY playing golf is not exercise have never been caddies.

Also, people who sneer at the amount of physical effort required in a round of golf are people who don't play golf or people who define exercise as running a marathon.

A full golf swing uses nearly every muscle in the body.

The head bone is connected to the neck bone, and so forth, on down to the bottom of the feet, and almost every connection is called upon to perform in the hitting of a golf ball.

There definitely are golf muscles that must be developed if you are to hit the ball far and with authority, but even the weakest swing uses the feet, the legs, the hips, the shoulders, the arms and hands.

If you walk eighteen holes around the course, give yourself credit for a brisk stroll of five or six miles. If you carry your own bag or pull it in a trolley, give yourself a little extra credit on your calorie-burning chart.

Even if you ride in a golf car, you will put in a couple of miles standing and moving on your feet that I would call exercise.

Scientists have figured out that a full swing with a driver by a good player uses about four horsepower of energy.

The full swing of a good player may look effortless and relaxed. But take a closer look at the player's face at the moment of impact. What you will see is anything but relaxation. The concentration is intense, the lips are tight, the teeth are gritted. The point of power is in the moment.

What you want in the golf swing is, as Jack Burke said, a feeling of controlled violence.

This definitely equates to exercise.

If you come home after a round and your mate says, "What you are tired for? All you did was play golf," I don't know how you can explain it or if you should even try. It's like trying to explain music to someone with a tin ear.

Betsy Rawls understood in her early days as a pupil and player that physical condition is very important to a golfer. Betsy got her sleep and ate a good diet, and the last six holes of nearly every match belonged to her.

In my opinion, playing golf is a fine way to exercise. Not only do you use your muscles, you use your mind. A good round of golf leaves you pleasantly satisfied physically, mentally, and emotionally.

Listen to the Swish

To UNDERSTAND WHAT clubhead speed means, turn your golf club upside down and grip it just below the clubhead and swing it hard and listen to the swishing sound it makes.

The swish is where the fastest part of your swing is.

You should hear the swish right at the ball—and beyond.

If you hear the swish early in your downswing, you are hitting from the top. Keep swinging until your swish is in the right place.

This sounds almost comical, but if I shorten your swing, your swish is going to be someplace different than it was when your swing was longer.

You have to concentrate on getting the maximum speed where the ball is. Listen to your swish to find out where you are.

There is no rule that says every practice swing on the golf course has to be the normal one with your clubface brushing the grass. Turn your club upside down and swish it a few times to find the feeling of speed and power.

Even when you are taking an upside-down practice swing, aim the butt of your club at a target on the ground and give it a healthy swish.

Alignment

To LINE UP a shot, I suggest you stand a few paces behind the ball and draw a picture in your mind of the line that runs from you through the ball and on to the target that you select. Make it a specific target. From the tee, aim at a certain spot of grass on the fairway rather than aiming just generally down one side or the other. Approaching the green, aim at exactly where you want your ball to drop, instead of merely aiming at the whole green.

Approach your ball from the rear and then turn to face it. Put the bottom of your blade at a right angle to the line. You neither close your blade nor open it.

Now take a small step sideways toward the target with your front foot, then a bigger step back with your rear foot. This places your ball a little to the left of center in your stance.

Take another glance toward your target and, without

wasting time for more than a waggle, go ahead and hit the ball while the picture is still clear in your mind.

Almost every good player lines up and fires pretty much this way.

On the practice tee, if you wish to check your alignment, place a club across your thighs. Where the club points is the direction you are aiming. This works on the golf course as well as on the practice tee, but it looks amateurish to do it while you are playing.

Sometimes, when a pupil asks where she is aimed, I answer her, "Hit a solid shot and it will tell us."

But We're Not Robots

PUPILS TELL ME they want to learn a swing they can repeat every time. "Like watching that Ben Hogan playing at Colonial," they will say. "He hits the ball the same way every time. He's a robot. That's how I want to be."

But if you asked Hogan how many of those swings he made at Colonial that day were just exactly alike, I imagine he would tell you none. If you asked how many of the shots out of the seventy that made up his round would satisfy him as being purely struck, he would probably say four or five.

To have a repeating swing is the goal of pupils who aspire to be good or better players.

This is as it should be. Yet we understand that the flowing of thought and movement that cause the swing is always different in some way from that of the swing preceding it.

One reason is that in golf we never have the same shot twice. You may have played a hole a thousand times, but you will never have exactly the same lie, the same grass, the same breeze, the same temperature and humidity, the same energy, the same vision, the same blood sugar level, the same distance to the pin, the same unrepaired divot unseen on the green, and be exactly the same age—all these things come together in different combinations and prevent any two shots from being exactly the same.

Thus we adapt a swing that is constantly changing in tiny, unnoticed ways to the demands of a shot that we have never actually hit before.

And when something really strange happens to the shot, good or bad, we say, "That's golf." Because how else could we explain it? Robots can perform some aspects of the game, but it requires the human mind to complete the package.

Home

WHAT A BEAUTIFUL place a golf course is. From the meanest country pasture to the Pebble Beaches and St. Andrews of the world, a golf course is to me a holy ground. I feel God in the trees and grass and flowers, in the rabbits and the birds and the squirrels, in the sky and the water. I feel that I am home.

Compliment from the Haig

DURING HIS BARNSTORMING days of matches and exhibitions all over the United States and Europe, proud members of the clubs Walter Hagen was visiting would always ask what he thought of their golf courses.

Hagen was a master salesman, at ease in any company, the person who made being a golf professional into a respected occupation.

His answer to the question regarding what he thought of the golf courses was, "In my opinion, this is without a doubt one of the finest courses of its type that I have ever played."

Checking Ball Position

BALL POSITION IS an easy thing to lose. One day it is right, and you are striking the ball solidly, and the next day you are slicing or pulling your shots without realizing that your ball position has changed.

Where the ball is played in your stance and how far you are standing from it at address are vital to a good golf game.

Shelley Mayfield, an old friend and pupil who was a good tour player and later became a top club pro at Brook Hollow, had an excellent idea of how to check his ball position.

Once, during a period when he was hitting the ball especially well, it occurred to Shelley to get a big piece of cardboard and draw on it the position of his feet and the position of the ball.

From then on, if anything started going wrong, Shelley could haul out the cardboard and place his feet on it and see if ball position was the problem.

This is such a good idea that I think everyone should do it.

Remembering Babe

I PLAYED WITH Babe Didrickson in her first exhibition after she signed a contract with Wilson and turned pro. Al Espinosa, a Ryder Cup player, was with us.

Babe was a female counterpart of Arnold Palmer. Babe was bold and confident. She hit the ball far. Galleries loved her.

In that first exhibition, Babe hit a 7-iron thin, and her ball skidded over the green. She turned to me and said in a loud voice, "Harvey, these greens aren't holding very well today, are they?"

Babe could tell the rest of the players in a tournament that she was going to beat their socks off and make them like it, because she was not only telling the truth, she was also drawing the most fans.

She was a great athlete in all sports and had a natural, powerful golf swing. In the lessons I had with her, I could, in all honesty, mostly just watch in admiration as she innately seemed to know how to hit every shot in the book.

The day after she won the silver medal in the high jump at the 1932 Olympics, Babe was invited to play golf with some famous sportswriters—Paul Gallico, Grantland Rice, Westbrook Pegler, and Braven Dyer. They talked her into taking up the game seriously. She hit a thousand practice balls a day while making a living as a stenographer and pitching baseball for the bearded House of David teams in exhibitions. In 1934 she burst onto the golf scene as a genius and a crowd pleaser. She won her third U.S. Open in 1954 following surgery for the cancer that killed her two years later at the age of forty-five.

Babe married wrestler George Zaharias, and they had a happy wedded life. When I saw George shortly after her funeral, we both broke down and wept in each other's arms.

Know Your Own Game

NO ONE SHOULD know better than you whether you can hit a certain shot or not. Do not let yourself be overly influenced by the choice of clubs used by your companions. If it looks like a 6-iron shot to you but the others in your foursome are hitting 8-irons, you go right ahead with your first choice. It's getting the ball on the green and close to the hole that counts, not ego.

Once you do decide on the distance and the club, believe in your own decision and put your best swing on the ball. Keep doubt out of the picture. Betsy Rawls was the best woman player I ever saw at this facet of the game. If she ever doubted herself, you would never know it.

Howdy Do

EXPLAINING THE TURN to my pupil Gene Kirksey one day, I did it in such a way that she still laughs about it, and, most important, she remembers it.

I said, "Gene, just stand facing me. Now turn to your right as if someone had just walked up beside you, stick out your right hand to shake hands with that person, and say, 'Howdy do.'"

She started laughing, but she did it.

"Howdy do," she said, sticking out her hand.

"Now," I said. "Someone has just walked up from your left. Turn all the way back around and stick out your right hand to shake hands with that person and say, 'Howdy do.'"

Gene did it. "Howdy do," she said, shaking hands with the imaginary person on her left.

Gene tells me thinking about Howdy Do right and then Howdy Do left has made the golf turn forever clear in her mind.

Howdy do . . . howdy do. You might want to try it.

Playing Pregnant

ANNIE NELSON, WHOSE husband, Willie, is the famous singer and songwriter, has had two sons in the last few years, and each time she kept playing golf almost right up to the moment they rushed her to the hospital.

The more heavily pregnant Annie became, the smoother her swing became and the bigger turn she made.

I mentioned this to Cindy Figg-Currier, who was in her sixth month of pregnancy at the time.

"It's the same way with me," Cindy said. "I feel that my center of gravity is steadier, and I really have something to make my turn around."

The only danger I can imagine in playing pregnant is if you overdo it and get too tired. Otherwise, carry your little passenger around the course and enjoy yourself. Who knows? You might be training a future world champion.

Patty's First Time

JIMMY DEMARET AND I played with Patty Berg and another woman, whose name is lost in my memory, in Patty's first professional exhibition match.

It was a bitter cold day with the wind howling, and only a few Eskimos showed up to see the golf.

Jimmy and I wanted to call it off. Little Patty said nothing, but her father insisted that we get out there and play as we had promised.

Oh, what a dreadful front nine! My hands turned blue. The wind whipped my scarf against my face. Jimmy was having no more fun than I was. Patty marched bravely onward accompanied by her caddie and her father.

As we reached the turn, even the Eskimos had gone away.

The Ladies Golf Association at the
Austin C.C., c. 1935. Helen is second from left, standing.

But Patty's father was very insistent that she not quit, so Jimmy and I trudged with her to the tenth tee box. The tenth was a downhill par four with the wind at our backs. Jimmy hit one solid and nearly drove the green. I was a few yards behind him, and Patty was quite a few more yards behind me, because she had hit her tee ball a glancing blow.

My teeth were chattering and my nose was running as I watched Patty addressing her iron shot, with her father urging her to do better.

Patty struck her iron. The ball bounced once on the front of the green and then rolled into the hole for an eagle.

I picked up the ball and said, "Nobody can do it any better than that. Patty, you're a great player and you're going to have a fine career."

Jimmy loudly and sincerely agreed, and we shook hands all around, and then Jimmy and I started walking back to the clubhouse on numb feet.

After a minute, Patty and her father came along behind us. I guess he was disappointed that his daughter's first professional exhibition was incomplete, but I knew Patty would show him wonderful golf for many years to come.

PART IV

from
*The Game for
a Lifetime*

Foreword

THIS IS THE BOOK Harvey Penick was preparing when he fell ill with pneumonia in the spring of 1995. He passed away with Tom Kite at his bedside on a Sunday afternoon one week before Ben Crenshaw won a second Masters Championship in what seemed a supernatural manner, as if the spirit of his mentor had entered his mind and heart to guide him to this triumph.

Only two weeks earlier, again on a Sunday afternoon, Harvey had given the final lesson of his more than seventy years as a teaching pro. From his deathbed, the ninety-year-old Penick spoke hoarsely as Crenshaw stroked balls on the carpet, using a hickory-shafted Sarazen putter that was kept in the corner for lessons to pilgrims who came to the house seeking aid.

Ben placed his hands on the old putter, and Harvey began reminding Crenshaw of the boyhood stroke they had known together, a silky touch that has made Ben one of the finest putters in the history of the game.

"Trust yourself. Believe in yourself," the old master said.

When it was time for Ben to take his wife, Julie, and their two daughters home so Harvey could try to rest, the pupil leaned forward and kissed the master on the forehead and said, "I love you, Harvey."

"I love you, too, Ben. I'll be watching you always."

Ben swallowed hard, and his eyes misted. "I know you will," Ben said.

As he turned to leave the bedroom for what they knew

would be the last time, there was a look on Ben's face as if an electric shock had struck his soul.

During the following week, Harvey had brief periods when he could breathe without the oxygen tube in his nose, and the pain in his back diminished, and he talked of returning soon to the practice range. He was excited at the prospect of giving lessons to country music legend Willie Nelson. Willie had signed "You Saved My Game" on the brim of a cap that Harvey wore.

Harvey urged visitors to look at his Willie cap and also at what had come in the mail—an Indiana University basketball autographed "To A Great Teacher," and signed "Bob Knight."

"I think I can help Willie," Harvey would say with a smile. "I hope it's not too late. I don't mean too late for Willie's game. I mean too late for me in general."

During those good periods, Harvey would bring up the new book he had been concentrating his efforts toward. He could no longer write legibly, though he continued to turn out pages until near the end. Every visit, no matter if he felt better or bad, he asked if I was certain his notes and letters were in a safe place.

He had given me three shoeboxes of papers and had urged me to dig through the larger boxes in the garage and through the folders in his briefcase, where among other treasures I found the attested scorecard from 1985 when University of Texas women's golf coach Susan Watkins, at that time an assistant pro at Austin Country Club, shot a women's record 73 from the men's Gold championship tees at the club's new Pete Dye course. The scorecard had been lost in Harvey's briefcase for a decade.

His final book, Harvey said, was for what he called seasoned players. By seasoned, Harvey meant golfers who had played the game earnestly for no telling how many years.

He believed you could be seasoned at fifteen or at ninety-five, depending on the intensity of your experience with the game.

Harvey's purpose in making his final book was to entertain and enlighten seasoned players, reveal to them his beliefs, and encourage them to continue their romance with the most mysterious, most cerebral, most frustrating and supremely satisfying of all games that can be played by one person alone.

One morning on the practice range at Austin Country Club, months before pneumonia invaded him, Harvey had laughed when I repeated a remark I had heard from Waxo Green, the late Nashville sportswriter. Waxo had said, "You know you're getting old when all your irons start going the same distance."

Harvey nodded and grinned. Later, I saw him writing a note called "Waxo's Puzzle." In the next few days he started scribbling in notebooks and on scraps of paper.

Some pages were memories of experiences he'd had with friends and pupils. Some were a few sentences that told Harvey's points of view on playing golf, on learning the lessons of the game, on keeping in mind the joys and benefits of it in the face of the despair it can cause. He had been reminded of stories about club members and other golf pupils, including professionals, that always involved an instructional point and usually a smile. He felt that the heart of his teaching—Take Dead Aim—had not been fully understood by some, and he added to the explanation he had given in his *Little Red Book*.

His shoeboxes became stuffed with notes on and letters from seasoned players from all over the world with handicaps from less than zero to more than 30, with a range in age of about eighty years. He read the letters with a magnifying glass.

Harvey and Bud Shrake, 1993.

Harvey meant this book for those who have advanced into the mysteries of the game and may find his words helpful in understanding their obsession.

Harvey wrote his last note on Friday, March 3, after lecturing to an audience of amateurs, mostly high handicappers, who had gathered to hear him at the Golfsmith teaching academy that bears his name in north Austin.

His young nurse would huddle close beside him during these lectures and translate the questions from the audience for him. Harvey could barely hear. His hearing aids squealed. But he could understand the nurse's voice and was good at reading lips. Harvey loved these sessions. He said seeing the people laughing at his jokes and stories made him feel like Bob Hope or Jimmy Demaret.

That Friday evening the congestion in Harvey's lungs grew severe and the EMS was called to take him to St. David's Hospital, where his wife, Helen, had worked as a volunteer for many years.

On a stretcher in the ambulance, Harvey peered up into the eyes of a young paramedic. Harvey had never seen him before, but he recognized a seasoned player.

"You're a golfer, aren't you, son?" Harvey wheezed.

"Yes, sir." The paramedic hesitated. This might not seem like the right time. But, then again, when might he ever have another chance like this?

"Mr. Penick, would you please check my grip?"

Harvey gladly did so, for teaching was his joy. He pronounced it a good grip and told the paramedic to use it without fear and enjoy his game.

Then he beckoned the young man to bend close because Harvey's voice was growing faint.

"Remember to leave my share of your winnings in the pro shop," Harvey said. He smiled. That was a little joke he used with pupils for decades. He didn't expect anyone to do it, and they understood.

After seven days in the hospital, Harvey was sent home to die. He needed nurses around the clock. On his first day after returning to the house he shared with Helen on Fawn Creek Path, Harvey sat for a while in his wheelchair in the sunlight on the rear deck where he could see flowers and birds and squirrels and sense the water running over rocks in the creek bed below. He autographed a few of the hundreds of books that were stacked up and waiting. He read some of his mail. His strength began failing, and he asked to be put to bed where he lay for the rest of his life.

For the next three weeks, the Penick home was open to a stream of visitors. Harvey was always cordial, despite his illness. But he was growing weaker and more frail. In his prime, Harvey weighed 135 pounds. Now he had wasted down to 84. One morning when I entered his bedroom, Harvey was writing in a notebook. Seeing me, he shook his head. "I can't do it anymore," he said. He showed me the notebook. The page was covered with circles and scrawls. "I know what I'm trying to say, but this pen won't say it."

I thought Harvey was going to pass over on the Sunday that Ben and Julie Crenshaw and their daughters came to see him. Harvey had been trying to talk to me, but his breath was rasping and his lips refused to form words. When I met Ben at the front door, I said, "You'd better hurry."

A few minutes later, I was surprised to see Harvey roll over on one elbow and hear him loudly and distinctly say, "Go get the putter," to begin the last lesson with Ben.

Harvey fought off death several times in the next week. He was exhausted and in terrible pain, but he was determined to be at Austin Country Club on Sunday, April 2, for the unveiling of a bronze statue of Harvey and Tom Kite.

When sculptor Don Davis asked his permission, Harvey replied, "I've never done anything to deserve me being made into a statue."

Davis then asked Kite, U.S. Open Champion and at that time golf's all-time leading money winner. Kite answered, "I've never done anything to deserve me being made into a statue beside Mr. Penick."

By Saturday night, Harvey realized he would not be able to endure the journey of a few blocks from home to the club. He was clinging to life purely by willpower. He told friends who had gathered around him that he wanted the unveiling to be an occasion of celebration, not of mourning.

On Sunday afternoon, a musical ensemble played for a crowd on the lawn beside the clubhouse. The wrapping was removed from the statues. Revealed were two standing figures—Harvey as mentor studying the swing of pupil Kite. The teacher and the pupil gaze through the oaks down toward the first tee and the river.

In a sometimes trembling voice, Kite told the crowd, "When I am asked what is the biggest break I ever had in golf, I say it is when the IRS transferred my dad from the Dallas office to Austin. Because I arrived in Austin at age thirteen to encounter Mr. Penick and Ben Crenshaw. In my wildest dreams, I couldn't have hoped for a finer teacher or stronger competition."

The moment the ceremony ended, I went back to Harvey's bedroom with his lawyer, Richard Pappas, and we described the event. Harvey raised up as nearly as he could and grasped my hand with both of his and said, "I'm going to die now. I'm ready."

Kite came in a short while later. He had lingered at the club to be gracious to the crowd, as Harvey would have wanted. Tom sat and held his old teacher's hand and told him about the unveiling. Harvey asked how Davis Love III was doing at the tournament at that moment in New Orleans. The late Davis Love, Jr., himself a great teacher, had been one of Harvey's favorite pupils on the University of Texas golf team and had played in the Masters as an amateur. Now the son needed to win in New Orleans to get an invitation to the Masters the next week.

Tom went into the living room, where family and friends were watching on the large color TV. Kite returned and told Harvey that Davis was in a playoff for the title in New Orleans. Harvey smiled and lifted his thin arms up to his face and clapped his palms together three times.

Shortly past five o'clock, Harvey's son-in-law, Billy Powell, entered the bedroom with the news that Davis Love III had won the tournament in New Orleans and qualified for the Masters. Sometime in these seconds, Harvey's soul passed on to somewhere else. "But I know Mr. Penick knows Davis won. I'm sure of it," Tom said at once.

Using his cellular phone out on the Penicks' deck above the creek, Kite called Crenshaw, who was having dinner in Augusta. It was the call Ben had been dreading. The two champions, both of them as bound to their teacher as sons to a father, made a plan. Kite would go to Augusta on Monday morning. He and Crenshaw would play practice rounds Monday and Tuesday. On Wednesday morning they would charter a plane to fly back to Austin to be pallbearers at Harvey's funeral.

Ben hadn't been playing well. He had missed the cut in a tournament, which is how he could be at the Penick house on the Sunday of the putting lesson two weeks before that final round at the Masters.

While Ben was hitting practice balls at Augusta National and making himself accept that he would soon be carrying Harvey's coffin, caddie Carl Jackson, who always handles Ben's bag at Augusta, spoke up to him, "Why don't you move the ball back a little in your stance, and then make a tighter turn with your shoulders."

Ben tried Jackson's suggestion. In just a few swings, Ben began hitting the ball as solidly as he had ever hit it. His confidence returned, and his youthful, graceful, classic swing along with it.

At a surprise party in Austin to celebrate Crenshaw's second Masters championship, both of them won with Carl Jackson on his bag, I asked the tall, thoughtful Jackson why it had occurred to him to offer Ben the advice that he did.

"I don't know exactly," he said. "I was watching him closely, and the words just suddenly were revealed in my mind what I must say to him."

It rained hard on the morning of the funeral, but the private plane from Augusta flew through the storms carrying Ben and Julie Crenshaw, Tom and Christy Kite, golf teacher Chuck Cook, and Terry Jastrow, the ABC-TV golf producer who had once become Texas Junior Golf Champ under Harvey's guidance. Harvey's admirers packed the funeral home, many standing outside under umbrellas to be part of the service.

At the cemetery, Kite and Crenshaw, tears running down their cheeks amid the raindrops, helped to place their mentor's coffin in the shelter of the tent that protected the grave. Each of them laid a flower on top of the casket and bowed his head.

The sun came out as the Augusta party flew back that afternoon. On the following morning, Ben began his march toward the Masters title that captured the emotions of millions who watched it actually happen. It was an event that made sport universal, timeless, and important. It was a parable of fathers and sons, of learning and teaching, of love and trial and inspiration and revelation, and perhaps a glimpse beyond the curtain.

During the final nine holes at Augusta on Sunday, the emotional tension grew thicker than the smell of southern pines and magnolias. Ben had said he was going to win the

Masters for Harvey. Television and newspapers had played major stories linking Ben with the spirit of his mentor.

On everyone's mind was the awed question: Can this really be happening? When an errant shot by Crenshaw hit a tree but bounced into the fairway, a TV commentator said, "I bet Harvey Penick kicked that ball back in."

With Davis Love III tied for the lead up in front of him, Crenshaw hit a 6-iron as well as one can be struck at number sixteen, the seventieth hole of the tournament, then made a tricky, heart-stopping putt for a birdie. On the seventeenth green, Ben stroked a wide breaking putt across the slick grass into the cup for another birdie and a two-stroke lead over Love. At that point, Ben had needed only nine putts for the last eight holes. Remarkably, in four rounds he would not three-putt even one of Augusta National's greens, all of which are famously fast and deceptive.

After he holed out at the seventy-second hole for a one-shot victory, Ben bent and buried his face in his fingers for a moment, and then he lunged into the embrace of Carl Jackson and wept on the chest of the man who had carried his bag, and who had been inspired to reveal a few crucial words of advice at exactly the right moment.

All over the country people were watching that drama at the Masters on television and weeping with the sheer thrill of it, and everywhere people were thinking, Yeah, I do believe in angels.

Ben told the press, "I could definitely feel him with me. I had a fifteenth club in my bag. The club was Harvey." After the Masters, Ben wrote a letter to Tinsley Penick that said, ". . . it gives me great pleasure to know that what your father tried to tell his pupils works not only today but for the rest of one's life."

It went largely unremarked in the excitement and wonder of Ben's second Masters, but in 1984 Ben had consulted Harvey for guidance before leaving for Augusta and had

*"Angels at Augusta"—painting by Paul Milosevich,
honoring Harvey and Bobby Jones as Ben Crenshaw's
inspiration for the 1995 Masters.*

followed by winning his first Masters Championship in an enormously popular and sentimental victory.

In his introduction for Harvey's *Little Red Book,* which was published two months before Tom Kite won the 1992 U.S. Open at Pebble Beach, Crenshaw wrote that in many ways Harvey reminded him of the fabulous Scotsman Old Tom Morris, the philosopher from St. Andrews. Old Tom, Ben wrote, lived a fulfilling life knowing he contributed to others' enjoyment of the game.

Ben wrote: "Old Tom was wise, treated all men equally, and kept things very simple. It did not take much to make him happy. As long as he was around his many friends, and there was golf to be played and talked about, he was truly *contented.* Many times Old Tom would say 'I've got mae God and mae gowff to see me thro.'"

Harvey might well have said that, too, but in his Texas drawl. These are his last words on golf and on life.

—Bud Shrake
Austin, Texas, 1996

The Dreamer Sees the Real Thing

A FELLOW DROVE into the parking lot of our Pete Dye course beside the river. He parked his Mercedes-Benz with California plates in the shade of our live oak trees and walked into the golf shop and asked to see my son Tinsley, the head pro.

This visitor was a good-looking man with an athletic build. His clothes were top quality. His shoes were shined.

His face glowed with health. Tinsley invited him into the grill room so they could have a glass of iced tea at a comfortable table while he waited to hear what the man wanted.

"When I was a kid, I was a terrific player," began his story. "Junior championships, state high school champ, played for a university team that did well in the nationals. Got married my senior year. I wanted to try the pro tour, but instead I started in sales for my father-in-law's company and made more money playing golf with clients my first year than any rookie on the pro tour made grinding his heart out.

"I've kept my game in good shape. My handicap is a traveling 4. In the last year, I've had a 68 at the Old Course, a 70 at Pebble Beach, a 70 at Pine Valley, for example, and there was one great day when I shot a 67 at Riviera. For a CEO who has made more money than he knows what to do with, and also has a handsome wife and family, I can really play golf."

Tinsley congratulated him on his success.

"But I'm not satisfied," the fellow said.

"Why not?" Tinsley asked.

"I still want to play on the pro tour."

Tinsley drank his tea and waited.

"This is no pipedream," the fellow said. "I'm talking about the Senior Tour. I'm forty-three years old. I have sold my company for a very large sum. I'm free now to do whatever I want. My plan is to move my family here and buy a house beside your golf course.

"Every morning for the next seven years I will show up on your doorstep, rain or shine. I want daily lessons from you, and I'd like your father to check me every week or so. I'll hit five hundred practice balls a day. I'll play golf every day from the tips on this very tough course. Soon as I reach the age of fifty, I'll turn pro and join the Senior Tour. I'll pay you and your father whatever you ask, if you'll agree to get me ready. What do you say?"

Tinsley didn't need long to think it over.

"Let me tell you about one of our club members," Tinsley said. "Like you, he's forty-three years old, and he's made all the money he'll ever need. He has a handsome wife and family. He practices golf every day, and he plays golf nearly every day. He's getting ready for the Senior Tour in seven more years. At this tough golf course, his handicap is a plus-4. He is your competition. He is the player you are going to have to learn to beat if you are going to go on the Senior Tour. I really don't want to spend seven years of my life trying to help you to do that. Not for any price.

"There's the man I'm talking about—he's sitting over by the window, eating a club sandwich."

Tinsley gestured toward Tom Kite.

Keeping the Edge

IN THE YEARS when Tom Kite and Ben Crenshaw were going around our Austin Country Club course near Riverside Drive nearly every day, I would say we had as many low-handicap players as any club in the country.

I was walking toward the practice tee one morning when I overheard a guest telling one of our members, "I don't get it. Why do I see all these good players out here taking lessons and practicing? What a waste of time and money. If I was a good player, I'd skip the lessons and practice and just go straight to the tee."

I wondered what this fellow might say to a great violinist. "Why bother with teachers and practice? You're such a good player, why don't you just play concerts only?"

I have known many golfers who could lay off the game for months at a time, maybe even for a year or more, and still go out and shoot in the 70s.

But I've never known one who could lay off for months and continue to play consistently at a championship level. Bobby Jones would rack his clubs in the storeroom for months in the winter and then he would go win an Open, but not without first taking time for intense practice sessions with his teacher, Stewart Maiden.

One of my scratch players left our club and moved to Kansas City. A couple of years later he came to me for a lesson.

Before we started, I asked what his problem was.

"My game is going downhill," he said. "I'm playing to a 3 handicap now. I want to get back to scratch and stay there."

I watched him hit iron shots for about ten minutes. I handed him his driver, and he pounded the ball long and down the middle.

"Well?" he said. "What am I doing wrong?"

"How often do you play golf?" I asked.

"Once a week is all I have time for anymore."

I said, "There's the answer. You need to play more. It's unreasonable for you to play once a week and expect to stay at scratch. From what I've seen today, you hit the ball as well as ever. But no once-a-week player can expect to maintain the scoring touch you need for scratch golf."

"There's nothing you can do for me?" he said.

I said yes, there was something I could do for him. I would go to the shop and line up a game for him with some other good players.

"This is the medicine you need," I said. "And you'll enjoy it while you're taking it."

Leaping Lucifer

THERE WAS A LOUD thunderstorm during the night.

Lightning cracked a limb off one of the giant oak trees that helped to make our golf course near Riverside Drive such a joy. We had many oaks I couldn't wrap my arms halfway around. They called our country road Riverside Drive because it followed the course of the Colorado River through the southeast part of town, but the road had been a cattle trail, and our golf course had been a dairy farm. A golf course needs water and good soil. The rolling farmland was excellent soil, and the thunderstorm was bringing us water. That night four or five inches of rain pounded the roof of our house a few yards from the twelfth tee.

Lord knows, we needed the rain. I never in my life complained about rain. Texas always needs rain, even when it is flooding. All natural-born Texans who have been on earth a while have endured long spells of no rain and have learned that a lot of rain always beats a drought.

At first light, I watched from our kitchen window, looking down the fairway to the green of the par-three twelfth as the rain stopped. I knew the lone creek that meandered through the course would be churning along out of its banks, and the caddies would be swimming in the ponds that formed in the swales. It would be at least noon before we could open for play.

There was plenty of work to do at the club, but I decided the rain had given me freedom to slip off and hit a bag of balls. I had a couple of lessons to give in the afternoon, and

I wanted to practice my trick shots that I showed off at clinics and in exhibitions at baseball parks. Some of my pupils, especially the girls, would ask me to hit trick shots for them, and I needed to keep my touch.

I put away my polished shoes and my trousers with the fresh-pressed creases that I ordinarily wore to the club, and dressed in old clothes that wouldn't be ruined by the mud. By nine o'clock, my shop duties were under control, so I sneaked out to the tenth fairway with a bag of balls. I wanted to practice, not draw a crowd and wind up doing a show.

I dumped a mound of balls in the wet grass, paced off 145 yards down the fairway, and dropped the shag bag to be used as my target.

I had been hitting 7-irons for about five minutes when I noticed someone was leaning against a pecan tree, watching me from under the dripping branches.

A muddy Cadillac was parked on Grove Road, which runs beside the tenth fairway. I was already losing my hearing, and I wasn't aware the Cadillac had arrived.

"They told me up at the club that Harvey Penick might be down here," the fellow called from under the pecan tree branches.

"That's me." I was really wanting to practice, but this fellow was nobody from around Austin, and he caught my eye because he looked a little bit like the movie actor W. C. Fields.

Walking toward me, the fellow said, "I heard Harvey Penick is a classy dresser," as if my old clothes made him doubt he was talking to the right person.

I addressed the ball with my clubface upside down and backward. It appeared impossible to hit a shot from that position. But I whacked a neat little draw that bounced up next to the shag bag.

"Good trick. I saw the Fat Man do it in Florida. You spin the grip in your hands faster than my eyes can follow it. Very nice," he said.

I looked the fellow over again. Bill Mehlhorn had told me about a big money player in Florida named the Fat Man.

"What's your name?" I asked.

"At my home club the boys call me Leaping Lucifer."

I smiled at that, but he didn't.

The fellow's nose wasn't as large as the movie actor's, but his face was flushed and plump with the expression of an angry baby. He was wearing a white silk shirt under a yellow cashmere sweater, and his trousers were creamy wool. He had on brown alligator shoes exactly like the pair I had left in the closet at home that morning. He was about the same age I was at the time, about fifty.

"I was hoping to get a lesson from you," he said. "I've driven all the way from New Orleans."

I said I could fit him in later in the day. He shook his head.

"I was hoping you could do it right now," he said. "I'm driving back this afternoon. I have a game at the club tomorrow morning. Please, pro, can I get my sticks out of the trunk? Tomorrow is my birthday, and I want to win."

"I don't promise I can help you," I said.

Before the words were out of my mouth, Leaping Lucifer was slogging across the fairway through the mud toward his Cadillac. I watched him open the trunk and wrestle with a leather bag that was big enough to carry three boys and a dog.

"Just bring your 7-iron," I yelled.

But he was already staggering back across the fairway, bent under the weight of the bag full of clubs, his alligator shoes squishing in the wet earth with each step. Mud was splashed all over his slacks and sweater. When he planted the bag beside me, it must have lowered three inches into the ground.

"Tomorrow's your birthday, is it?" I asked, to start him talking. Whatever demon had caused him to drive from New Orleans to Austin to seek help from a stranger, it might reveal itself if he talked about his life.

"Yeah. My fiancée is throwing a big party at the club tomorrow night. She organized a birthday tournament for me tomorrow afternoon."

"She sounds like a wonderful person," I said.

"I'm playing two guys a thousand bucks three ways, and five hundred with the other," he said.

I said, "I think you've come to the wrong teacher."

"I checked you out. You're the one. Dutch Harrison told me."

I said, "I'm happy to try to help you with your swing, but I've been known to fail, and I want no responsibility for what you win or lose at the tournament tomorrow. You'd better try a different pro."

"I didn't come to you because of the gambling money!" he cried, earnestly enough to make me believe him. "I came because I'm tired of being laughed at! Especially tomorrow! I don't want to be laughed at in front of my fiancée on my birthday!"

"What is it about you that is supposed to be so funny?" I asked.

"It's my golf swing!"

There was such misery and pleading in his voice that I told him to take out his 7-iron and address a mud clod as if it were a golf ball. His left-hand grip was very weak, rolled almost under the handle. With his right hand, he held the club like a sledgehammer. Otherwise, his address was all right. He stood to the clod in a plain way, as I like to see.

"Make a few practice swings," I said.

He swung the club back and around at shoulder height, like a baseball bat. I was about to inform him that a true practice swing is always aimed at some spot on the ground so that it will imitate golf, but curiosity made me move on quickly to placing a golf ball on top of the mud clod.

"Hit it," I said.

The violent motion that followed startled me into dropping my club.

Maybe I can compare it to a man with an axe attacking a charging wild beast.

The fellow slashed his right shoulder and arm viciously toward the clod, and at the same time he lunged forward far past the ball—and yet, there was an explosion of mud, and I saw his 7-iron shot flying about six feet off the ground and slicing a little to bounce some ten yards short of my shag bag.

As a teacher with many years of experience, I have seen all sorts of leapers and lungers, but Leaping Lucifer was in a class by himself.

The most amazing thing about his swing was the exquisite timing that was necessary for him to produce a straight, usable, halfway decent 7-iron. Despite his plump cheeks and his middle-aged body, Leaping Lucifer was very talented as an athlete, or else he had just now been very lucky.

"Do it again," I said.

I stepped back a few feet to escape the shower of mud from his clubhead and his feet as he leaped and bashed the ball, his head finishing nearly waist high and two feet in front of his left leg.

But the ball landed within thirty feet of the first one.

"Can you hit your 7-iron like this consistently?" I asked.

"Yeah, pro. Pretty much. I don't hit the ball far, but I'm straight. Long carries over water or some kind of swamp or gully, those things kill me. I avoid those courses. I like a course where I can hit run-up shots."

Remembering Lucifer all these years later, it occurs to me that he couldn't finish the first two holes at our Pete Dye golf course on the bank of the river we call Lake Austin. Lucifer's worm burners would never cross our ravines and water hazards. Most golf courses built in the 1980s went away from the old-fashioned ground game and forced players to hit the ball high. It would require a lifetime overhaul for Lucifer to hit a shot of much height. He could probably make it around the Old Course at St. Andrews with a score reasonably close to his handicap, and he could have finished a round at our Hancock Park or Riverside Drive courses, but his card at our new Austin Country Club would be a couple of X's followed by a brisk stroll back to the clubhouse.

"Are you going to help me?" he asked.

"What would you like me to do?"

"You can teach me to keep my head behind the ball so I look a little more stylish."

What he was asking for would take months, if it could be done at all.

"How often do you play golf?" I asked.

"Every Wednesday afternoon and usually on Sunday."

He was probably a doctor or a dentist. As a teacher, I had his best interest at heart, as I would expect from a doctor or dentist who was treating me. But this was like waiting until your disease was incurable or your teeth were falling out of your head before you went to see a professional.

"Do you practice your golf?" I asked.

"I hit a few balls before I go to the tee, just to warm up."

"What is your handicap?" I asked.

"I'm a 16."

I must have looked surprised that it was so low, because he misunderstood and scowled at me.

"I used to be a 12," he said. "But I was much younger then."

*Drawing of Harvey by
LPGA Hall of Famer Betty Hicks.*

"How long have you swung at the ball this way?" I asked.

"Probably twenty-five years. I didn't take up the game until I could afford to join a country club."

He realized his alligator shoes were buried in the mud, and he pulled his feet free and moved to a patch of ground that was a little more solid. I knew he was waiting for me to do something wonderful for him, but I had already mentally discarded the things I would ordinarily do for a player who lunges. I would have started with his grip, but fixing this fellow's grip would have only made matters worse.

Leaping Lucifer glanced at his wristwatch

"Just a couple more questions," I said. "These men you will be playing with tomorrow, can you beat them?"

"Yeah. All of them outhit me a long way off the tee, but with my handicap I win a lot more than I lose."

"Are you a good putter?" I asked.

"One of the best. If I need to sink a six-foot putt on the eighteenth green to win, I'll make it."

As the golf coach at the University of Texas, I told my boys to beware of the opponent who had both a bad grip and a bad swing, because chances are he repeated his mistakes consistently and had learned how to score. This was my diagnosis of Leaping Lucifer. Anything I did in one lesson to change his grip or his swing would destroy what he already believed and would cause him to lose all his bets tomorrow, a sorry birthday present.

"Listen, pro, I'd like to get started here," he said. "It's a tough twelve hours back to New Orleans."

I needed to give this fellow some kind of gift, something that would make him feel better about himself without ruining the only good thing about his swing, which was that he did it the same way over and over with impeccable timing.

Reflecting on the situation, I remembered Leaping Lucifer had not asked me to improve his golf game. He had asked me to make his swing look stylish, that's all. It was vanity. He had been swinging this way for twenty-five years, and he had been laughed at for probably as long. But he was a winner, so he had borne the burden of his opponents' wisecracks because he was taking their money.

Now his fiancée had entered the picture, and tomorrow was his birthday. He didn't want to be laughed at in front of her.

"You're a very lucky man," I said.

"Yeah?" He eyed me suspiciously. "How?"

"Well, you've got a new Cadillac car and a cashmere sweater and a woman who wants to marry you, plus you've made it through life in apparent good health for another year."

"Skip the sermon, pro. Let's talk about my golf swing. What are you going to do about it?"

"Nothing," I said.

"You give up, huh? It's that bad, is it?"

I took off my cap and scratched my head.

"In fact, I wouldn't touch your swing because you are a golfing genius. Your swing is not funny, it is unique to your particular genius. You play golf only once or twice a week, and you don't spend hours on the practice range. To keep your game going at a 16-handicap level, and win money from your opponents with it, you must be a genius."

He was liking what he was hearing. It was making sense. Sure, I told him, if he had time to put in long practice sessions and play several days a week, as most of the best players did, he could get his game down into the high 70s. Good a putter as he was, his scores would only get better.

Leaping Lucifer was smiling at me now.

"If they laugh at you tomorrow, you just wink at your fiancée. She's a smart woman. She'll see that they're really laughing at themselves because they aren't good enough to beat you. You and your fiancée can have a fine laugh while you're counting your winnings."

"Ah, pro," he said, "I see what you mean. What do I care if these losers laugh? I'm the one who wins the game."

"One more thing," I said. "It's a tip for tomorrow and now on. When you hit pitch shots to the green, use your sand wedge, and grip it high on the handle, which prevents chili-dipping, and hold tight with the pinkie and ring fingers of your left hand so the blade won't turn over. This will take three strokes off your game tomorrow."

This advice couldn't possibly hurt, and it would help if he remembered to do it. This was something technical enough for him to put his mind on it and feel he had learned something.

"Hey, great, thanks," he said brightly.

He wiped the mud off his right hand and stuck it out. I shook it.

"How much do I owe you?" he asked.

"Send 20 percent of your winnings to the Salvation Army," I said. "I hope your wedding is blessed forever. And say hello to Dutch Harrison for me."

I turned back to the pile of balls at my feet. Behind me I could hear the clanking and puffing as he heaved the heavy bag over his shoulder, and then the slurping of those beautiful alligator shoes sloshing through the mud on the fairway as Leaping Lucifer marched again to his Cadillac.

The Cadillac backed up and made a U-turn on Grove Road and I watched the sprays of water thrown up by its wheels as he drove happily off toward New Orleans.

I faded a 7-iron that landed with a loud plunk against the shag bag. I laughed and wiped my hands with a towel. It was a great morning to be alive and be teaching, and there were another fifty balls to hit before I would need to go back to the shop. That warm, easy feeling is hard to explain, but it is better than riches to me.

The Barbed Wire Line

IF YOU ARE having trouble coming over the top a little bit, or you find a tendency to flinch from the blow and hit up on an iron shot, or your downswing is from too steep an angle, there is a mental picture that may cure your problems.

Imagine that there is a line of barbed wire that starts from far behind your ball and goes all the way to your target.

The barbed wire is a few inches off the ground in your imaginary picture. The wire passes over your ball and aims directly at where you want your ball to go.

You must hit the ball without lashing and scratching your club against the barbed wire. The only way you can do this is by swinging from inside to square to inside and by staying down with the shot at impact.

Give this a try on the practice range, not during a golf game. If you practice it, you won't need to think about it while you are playing—unless something goes wrong with your swing in the middle of a round. Then you might walk off by yourself a little way and make a few practice swings at a tee, imagining the barbed wire line.

One of the better amateurs the University of Texas produced, Kirby Attwell, told me that he still uses the barbed wire line in his mind during practice sessions at River Oaks in Houston, where Kirby has been club champion about ten times.

Imagining barbed wire makes some pupils nervous. To them, I say to imagine a line drawn on the ground that runs over the ball from behind and goes all the way to the target.

Swinging back and swinging down, you should feel you are inside the line.

Crushed by Crunch

A PUPIL NAMED Townsend from California told me this story one summer while I was teaching at Cherry Hills.

Townsend was playing in an amateur match-play tournament at North Berwick in Scotland. He hired a local caddie who was known as Crunch.

Townsend and Crunch set out on a practice round the day before the tournament. It was Townsend's first visit to North Berwick, and he was awed by treading the ground that had been walked on by many of the giants of the game since the invention of golf. I have heard Ben Crenshaw say he thinks North Berwick is one of the best courses in the world.

Townsend said his feeling of reverence crept into his game and elevated him to heights he didn't know he was capable of. With Crunch trudging along beside him, selecting clubs for him and pointing out the proper places to aim and reading the greens, Townsend played the finest round of his life. The wind blew hard off the sea, as it is supposed to at North Berwick, and rain showers struck a couple of times, but Townsend marched bravely through the elements and holed a birdie putt at the eighteenth to finish two over par.

Townsend gave Crunch a handsome tip and arranged to meet him at the North Berwick golf shop the next morning for the beginning of the tournament.

"Do you know this fellow called Liam Flaherty?" Townsend asked the caddie.

"Aye," said Crunch.

"Tell me about him," Townsend said.

"Ah, he's no good," replied Crunch in his East Lothian dialect. "He's no good with his driver. He's no good with his irons. He's no good with his putter. He's just flat no good at all."

Townsend beamed at this news. "Flaherty is my opponent in the first round tomorrow."

"Ah," said Crunch. "He'll beat you."

Rock Solid Putting

EVERY TIME I see a touring pro miss a short putt on television, I see a head moving.

The average player misses short putts because of poor speed, poor aim, and an off-center hit, as well as a moving head.

But the expert is a good judge of speed and line and is able to stroke the putter so as to hit the ball solidly; or he or she wouldn't be an expert.

Moving your head or your eyes on a short putt is a result of fear or of carelessness, and it is a fault that has lost many a tournament.

To the Finish

Stewart Maiden's famous advice to Bobby Jones that "you don't hit the ball with your backswing" has been on my lips with many pupils.

For sixty years I have seen a parade of high-handicap pupils who somehow learned the swing the wrong way around. Rather than learning that what counts is the way the club goes through the ball, these pupils seem to believe they will receive style points for a lovely backswing regardless of what happens next.

Once the backswing is set in a correct position, these pupils act as if the job is done rather than just begun, and all sorts of unnecessary movements follow. The club will probably go out and over, cut across the ball in a glancing blow with little power, and wind up somewhere about breast high, usually as the pupil struggles to keep balance.

Fascinated by a well-done backswing, the pupil congratulates himself and then turns the critical function of striking the ball over to random actions.

A proper finish is the bookend to a good backswing. If you swing to a nicely balanced follow-through, what happens to the ball in the hitting area will be a success.

There is no aspirin to give for this problem that will make everybody feel better in an hour.

I believe the best approach for a teacher faced with this situation is to start the pupil's swing at a good, high, balanced finish, and proceed backward.

This will take time. One lesson is not enough to begin curing this fault, so I would try to teach something different but helpful, like clipping the tee, unless the pupil would promise to practice hard and come see me again.

If the pupil is willing to put in the study and practice, I ask the pupil to pose in a perfect follow-through, elbows out in front of the body, facing the target with the left foot carrying all the weight, head up and eyes looking down range to follow a good shot.

Once the pupil gets the feeling of what a good finish position feels like, I say, "Now I want you to make a swing that concludes in this exact position. Pay no attention to your backswing for now. We don't care if it is too long or across the line or too short or just right. Just take the club back slowly and make a swing that finishes in this balanced follow-through position."

I repeat, "The good finish shows what has gone on before it."

At a teaching seminar years ago, a British pro demonstrated how he taught the swing by starting at the ball and pushing it forward with the clubhead until it rolled away and then the pupil went on into a full finish.

The pro said the backswing was a natural thing that would come easily once the pupil learned the route and destination of the foreswing.

Let me add that a teacher must watch that his pupil swings into a good finish that is real and not faked. I don't mind if the pupil falls back a little bit now and then, but I don't like to see one ever fall forward.

You may be thinking that when you watch golf on television, especially the Senior Tour, you see a lot of abrupt follow-throughs. But remember that these are experts with years of experience, and they know how to move the club through the hitting area, and also their backswings tend more toward three-quarters than full. In many golf shots the backswing and the forward swing are the same length.

But the Senior Tour is still the home of classic swings

that have stood the test of time, as well as classic sluggers who have been winners for decades.

Older players are always telling me they can't take the club back as far as they once did. But that's not really their problem. Their problem is they can't swing the club as far forward as they once did.

Take a golf club or a walking cane or a broomstick and pose in front of the mirror in your bedroom. Put yourself into the finish position that you see the experts finish in. Hold yourself there, weight on your left foot, belt buckle pointing to the target. You look as good as Ben Hogan, don't you? Enjoy it as if you are watching a long, powerful shot sail down the fairway. Memorize it, and take that feeling to the golf course with you.

A Good Day at Cherry Hills

DURING ONE OF the summers I taught at Cherry Hills, I was having a difficult time with a pupil whose downswing was coming over the top. I was using all my wiles to teach her how to bring her clubface into the ball from the inside to square and then back inside, but there was something in her head that kept her swinging from outside to inside.

We paused for a chat. On a pleasant, sunny day in Denver, I would sometimes give as many as twenty lessons. I preferred it this way, because I could spend as much or as little time with a pupil as I thought would help. Some pupils needed five minutes. There were others I spent ten hours with—not all in one day, to be sure—and sometimes still failed to put them on the right path.

The woman pupil and I walked over to get a drink of water at Cherry Hills. I asked her, "Might it be that there is something on your mind that is bothering you?"

She looked away, a worried frown crossing her face, and said, "Why would you ask?"

"I don't mean to be prying into your personal life," I said. "I'm wondering if you are too distracted to listen to what I have been telling you. If your mind is elsewhere right now, let's call it off and try again another day."

She said, "No, I'm fine, really. I'm trying to do what you say. I'm trying to stay behind the ball and keep my shoulders level in my swing and . . ."

As she paused for a sip of water, I asked, "When did I tell you to keep your shoulders level when you swing?"

"Wasn't that you?" she said. "Well, anyway, everybody knows you're supposed to."

We walked back to our place on the range. I asked her to hit another 7-iron for me.

Her downswing came over the top again, but now it was clear to me where the problem was.

"What is it that you swing your shoulders level with?" I asked.

"Well, you know. Level."

"Do you mean level as in level with the horizon?" I asked.

"Sure. Level as in horizontal. I was taught that swinging my shoulders level is a fundamental," she said.

I asked her to address another ball. I went around behind her and placed my hands on her shoulders.

"Listen to me and think about what I'm saying," I said.

I asked her to make a slow-motion swing while I kept my hands on her shoulders.

When she started her right shoulder around in line with the horizon in her forward swing, I gripped her shoulders tightly and said, "Stop."

I guided her again to the top of her backswing.

Harvey driving the range ball cart, 1974.

"You misunderstood the teaching to swing your shoulders on a horizontal level," I said. "Horizontal means your shoulders turn horizontal with your posture. Horizontal with your spine. Not horizontal with the horizon. Let's try it again."

With my hands on her shoulders, she bent forward from the hips and kept her back straight and went through a slow-motion swing.

When she turned into her follow-through, she smiled as if I had suddenly given her an incredible gift.

"That's it!" she said. "I understand! Level with my spine, not with the edge of the world!"

I stepped around in front again. I watched her settle into address. She struck her 7-iron smartly, swinging from inside to down the line and back to the inside.

It gave me a shiver of pleasure, and I moved on along the range to where another pupil was warming up, waiting for me. I loved those long summer days at Cherry Hills.

Ezar the Wizard

I PLAYED A LOT of golf with my old friend Joe Ezar, a wizard with a club in his hands. As a trick shot artist, Joe rated with Joe Kirkwood and Paul Hahn as the best. Ezar was a Texan, born in Waco, and he had the wanderlust. He was known all over the world for golfing skills that were mighty close to incredible.

Fans were always asking Ezar and Kirkwood and Hahn why they didn't win every tournament they entered. All three gave the same answer: "Because every shot in a tournament is not a trick shot. Hitting the ball straight is the hardest shot of all."

Ezar would take off for South America or for Europe without a dime in his pocket. He knew his uncanny ability to handle a golf club would be his ticket. Joe would stow away on an ocean liner, and when the ship was too far from shore to make him swim, he would introduce himself all around and begin doing his tricks on the deck. By the time the ship reached port, Joe would have a lot of new friends and a nice bankroll. His new friends would discover that he was nearly as good at cards as he was at hitting a golf ball. George Low used to say Joe Ezar was the real Titanic Thompson. I've played golf with both, and I wouldn't know which way to bet between them.

One summer during the Great Depression, Joe hopped a ship to Europe to do his shows and play in a few tournaments. What he did at the Italian Open that year became the talk of the golfing world.

Joe was competing in the tournament. In those times, they played thirty-six holes a day for two days. Joe was hired to do an exhibition of trick shots the evening before the final two rounds. As always, Joe drew a big crowd.

After his routine had astounded the audience, Joe went to the putting green. He dropped three balls on a slope about twenty feet above the hole. Joe told the crowd he would sink one of the three. He sank the third. Then he went to the downhill side of the hole, dropped the three balls twenty feet from the cup, and announced that he would sink the third putt.

Joe did it.

One of the onlookers was Henry Cotton, who had shot two 67s to set a course record and lead the tournament.

Within Cotton's hearing, someone told Joe it was a wonder the Texas boy didn't hold the course record, since he could hit such marvelous shots.

Joe asked the club president, who was the boss of the tournament, how much a 66 would be worth. The president said he would pay Joe $100. Joe began to bargain.

Finally Joe said, "I'll do a 64 for five hundred dollars."

Furthermore, Joe took a cigarette case from the president's pocket. On the inside of the case, Joe wrote down the scores he would shoot hole by hole to make his 64.

The next day Joe was followed by the tournament's biggest gallery. He came to the ninth hole needing a 3 for a 32. He was fifty yards from the cup in 2. Joe called the crowd's attention to his problem—and then he holed it out!

Joe shot another 32 on the second nine for his course record of 64. The president pulled out his cigarette case and read the numbers. Joe had done his record in the exact order he wrote down.

Henry Cotton said it was one of the most amazing occurrences he had ever heard of in golf. I would certainly second that opinion. Joe's 64 passed every player in the Italian Open field except Cotton, who won first money with a final 66.

Golf was Joe Ezar's means of seeing the world and standing people on their ears a long way from Wichita Falls.

Practice? What's That?

———

MY MEMBERS COME home from playing golf in England and Scotland for the first time, and they usually remark to me how odd it is to visit the old courses like Royal Musselburgh and Prestwick and North Berwick, and find no practice grounds.

"We change our shoes in the parking lot, and then we go straight to the tee, unless there's time to use the putting green," they say. "But there's nowhere to loosen up the grease. Why didn't those designers of those famous old courses mark off some ground where you can hit practice balls before you play?"

There are two good reasons—the balls and the clubs.

Those old courses were laid in the earth long before the modern golf ball and the steel-shafted club.

Even after the gutta perchas and other handmade balls were replaced by mass-produced balls that were more regular in performance, the golf clubs still had hickory shafts.

If you went to a practice ground and hit fifty balls with your hickory-shafted mashie, you would have to take your club back to your pro and hope he could bend and shave and hammer your shaft back into playing condition.

Until the sturdy steel shaft, golfers didn't practice. Oh, you might sneak off to an empty fairway and whack a few. But there was none of this five hundred practice balls a day that later became the routine for champions like Ben Hogan.

There's one thing, however, they still do practice at those old Scottish and English courses. They practice putting. On summer evenings when it stays light until an hour or two before midnight, whole families turn out for putting on the green in the town square.

Short Game Touch

AFTER WATCHING A PUPIL blade three or four chip shots clear across the back of the green from a yard in the front fringe, and then leave the next shot about six inches past his left foot, I remarked, "Well, I see one thing I am mighty happy about."

"What's that?" the pupil said.

"I'm happy you are not repairing my watch today."

Touch—which is knowing how far and how hard to hit the ball—can be learned by all but an unfortunate few. Sometimes those who at first seem to have no touch at all turn out to be the victims not of inability, but of a lack of mindfulness to the moment.

I say touch can be learned. I don't say touch can be taught.

The way you learn touch is by practice. There is no other way. I have seen players who are born with a natural sense of touch and can lay their chip shots dead as if it's the simplest thing in the world. But there are fewer of these than there are of unfortunates who have no inner guidance whatsoever.

In the great middle range of players, the best scorers will turn out to be those who consistently get into the cup in two, no more than three, strokes from about fifty yards or less from the green.

You can hook a drive into the tall grass and then turn it into a par if you will dig it out with a lofted club and follow with a good pitch or chip and putt. But if you muff a pitch or a chip, you have lost a stroke nearly every time.

Practice your pitches, chips, and long lag putts. Pay attention to what you are doing. Make note of how far back you took the club to hit the shot that made the ball fly a certain distance. Take the club back to the same place and do it again. Be sure it is no fluke. Believe in it. On days when your touch is poor, you can still remember a technical thing—such as how far the ball will fly when you take your wedge back waist high—and put it to use to make a decent shot, even though you feel like a total stranger to the game.

Put variety into your practice to keep your mind on it. You might stand at the cup and lob a golf ball underhanded as far as you can. Where the ball stops, that becomes your practice distance. Using a golf club, feel you are throwing the ball back to the hole. Then lob the ball in another direction down the fairway, and begin again.

A few of these sessions will cut half a dozen strokes off your score.

Yoga

A FEW OF my senior friends, seasoned players, have taken up the study of yoga, which is a practice that teaches complete and intense concentration of the mind, as well as artful, healthy stretching of the muscles and especially strengthening of the small muscles.

I can't imagine a more useful pursuit for a golfer than the study of yoga.

I believe the small muscles must combine with the big muscles to hit the ball far and straight. Look at John Daly with his huge turn and long windup. The big muscles of his back, hips, and legs pour the power into his violent swing, but it is the small muscles that make the snap and precision that launch those 350-yard drives. In my opinion, Daly is the most exciting player to come along in years. If he were to study yoga to calm his mind and tune his small muscles, there is no telling how good he could be.

I heard somewhere that Greg Norman, another power hitter and a great champion, is applying himself to Zen and to the martial arts to build his power of concentration.

In Zen they ask what is the sound of one hand clapping. Well, what you hear from me is the sound of two hands clapping at the idea of golfers delving into these ancient disciplines.

All seasoned players know, or at least have felt, that when you are playing your best, you are much the same as in a state of meditation. You are free of tension and chatter. You are concentrating on one thing. It is the ideal condition for good golf.

One of my longtime pupils told me recently that he meditates at the club. "I do it in the evenings on the practice range, hitting balls. It utterly calms my mind and leaves me refreshed," he said. "No telling how much hitting golf balls has saved me in psychiatrist bills. "

I have always taught that golf requires the kind of muscles that snap a whip rather than the kind of muscles that pick up a heavy barbell.

Except for the famous amateur Frank Stranahan, and a few others over the years, weightlifting has been frowned upon by the better players.

Now weightlifting has become acceptable and even encouraged. There is a trailer van that follows the pro tour carrying weightlifting machines and dead weights.

I suppose any exercise that strengthens the forearms and hands is probably good, as would be a turning exercise that builds muscles in the middle of the body.

Anything that strengthens your hips and legs is good, too.

In my mind, the best exercise is to swing a heavy practice club every day. I know swinging the heavy club builds the right muscles for golf.

Yoga is also the study of breathing. As I grow older, I reflect on how we take breathing for granted. Proper deep breathing is a joy, it makes you feel good, it calms your mind. Deep breathing is wonderful on the golf course as a provider of oxygen and strength throughout your body. I'll bet on a deep breather any time over a player who just breathes to stay alive.

With the stretching exercises that yoga teaches, you gain flexibility. If your body is flexible, you can keep playing good golf for your entire life.

I Wonder Why

THE GOOD PLAYERS are almost always the ones who ask me to watch them on the putting green. The high handicappers, who need it the most, had rather do anything than have a putting lesson.

Pick It Up

WHEN YOUR OPPONENTS concede you a gimme putt, you should show the courtesy to pick up your ball and walk away. There's always the player who says, "Aw, I'll just putt it for fun, anyway," and then misses and says, "That was only for practice."

They may not write it on the scorecard, but everybody knows down deep that the missed putt should have counted, and maybe they shouldn't concede any more to this player.

The Great One's Tricks

HARVEY VARDON HAD a habit of touching his right toe to the spot where his ball had been before his swing had sent it somewhere else.

After his follow-through, the great champion would look back down to the spot and touch it before he walked on.

I believe this was a well-thought-out piece of his technique. He was always reminding himself that the point of the swing is to hit a spot.

Vardon also carried a piece of chalk. He rubbed the chalk on the face of his club before he hit each shot. It was said he did it to help get backspin, but I believe Vardon was reminding himself to hit the ball on the chalk—the club-face.

He was a master. He knew you must hit what you swing at.

Jones's Rules and One More

BOBBY JONES SAID because tension is golf's worst enemy, he had set forth six rules that would help develop a freewheeling swing.

1. Grip the club lightly, mainly in the fingers, and make sure you can feel the clubhead.
2. In addressing the ball, arrange your posture as naturally and comfortably as possible.
3. Use the legs and hips in beginning the backswing, and swing the club back rather than picking it up with the hands and arms.
4. Be sure your backswing is long enough that your downswing will have time to get up speed before contact.
5. Start your downswing in a leisurely fashion, in no hurry coming down, with the acceleration smooth and natural.
6. When it comes time to hit, don't leap at the ball, but keep on swinging until the ball has had a good start down the fairway, and the clubhead has done its job.

To these rules, I would add one more for the average golfer—be sure your shoulders are square to the line.

Luck

To MY COLLEGE boys and to my other pupils who were heading into tournaments, I would always say, "Play well," instead of saying, "Good luck."

Like life, golf is a game of good breaks and bad breaks. There is nothing fair about it. But the person who plays well usually has a larger share of good breaks. The old saying is, "The more I practice, the luckier I get."

However, luck is out of our control. We can only try our best on each shot and keep on trying until the game is over. Luck will have its own way.

After thirty-eight holes of a semifinal match at the PGA at Olympia Fields, Leo Diegel and Walter Hagen came to the third tee all square.

Diegel bashed one of his powerful shut-face drives far down the fairway. Hagen, a swayer and lunger, hit a big slice over the trees and into the deep rough. Diegel had a simple approach to the green. As Hagen waded through the high grass toward his ball, it appeared he would have no chance to reach the green from his miserable position.

But arriving at his ball, Hagen found it sitting up nice and fat atop a perfect slab of turf being grown in a nursery that supplied patches for the greens.

Diegel was shaken to his toes by the sight of Hagen's second shot flying long and high over the trees and onto the putting surface. Leo managed to halve that hole with a par, but he topped his drive on the next tee and the match was soon finished.

Yes, a player must have a certain amount of luck to win a

*Kite and Crenshaw, co-medalists at the
1972 NCAA championships
for the University of Texas.*

major championship, but luck by definition is unpredictable. Don't count on luck to get you out of a tight spot. Better you do your best with each shot as it comes, and accept the luck however it falls.

A Word from the Wise

TOMMY KITE TOLD me that in a tournament one year at Harbour Town, he hit his second shot into the rear fringe of the green, a few feet beyond the putting surface.

Tommy reached back and his caddie, Mike Carrick, handed him the club he wanted to use for the chip shot, an 8-iron.

After carefully studying the chip, Tommy, who is one of the best chippers in the history of the game, drew back his club and chili-dipped the shot, moving the ball three feet.

Stunned, Tommy turned and stared at Mike.

"Well, I still believe that's the right club," Mike said.

Tommy laughed. These words of wisdom from his caddie and old friend put Tommy's mind back to the job at hand.

He took his stance again with the 8-iron and chipped the ball into the hole for a par.

Waxo's Puzzle

I HEARD ABOUT the lament of the Nashville sportswriter, Waxo Green, who said he could tell he was getting old because his iron clubs all carried the same distance.

This is not the fault of age. As you get older, you may expect to lose some distance with your irons, but the yardage between clubs should stay fairly constant.

The reason Waxo's irons all go the same distance is a lack of strength.

I see this among beginners, especially women, and older golfers who let their muscles get out of shape. These older golfers steadily descend to a level of not hitting the ball hard enough for the loft to make any difference. They are just clunking the ball with a hunk of steel. That's why their 4-irons go as far as their 8-irons.

It takes a hearty spank to make the ball go. The weak hand will not do it.

For anyone living with Waxo's Puzzle, I suggest stretching your muscles, doing flexibility exercises for a few minutes every day.

If you will do the stretching for five minutes in the evening and follow by swinging a weighted golf club for a short while, in a couple of weeks you will see a big change in your clubhead speed. I received a letter with a New York postmark, written on stationery from Winged Foot, that says, "Why do you keep harping on swinging a heavy club? You say it over and over. Surely with the many advances in golf technology, there must be a better way to build golf muscles other than swinging a heavy club. Swinging a heavy club is very boring."

Golf muscles are not for sale. If they were, golfers would pay almost any price. Golf muscles must be built and strengthened and then kept in tune. There are no shortcuts. Swinging a heavy club is not only the best way, it is the only way that I know that succeeds for sure.

Whether you have Waxo's Puzzle or not, swinging the heavy club a few minutes every day is a certain way to hit the ball farther.

Walter's Way

─────

WHEN I PLAYED an exhibition with Walter Hagen, it appeared to me that the great man would now and then drive his ball into the trees just so he could show the fans his genius at hitting recovery shots.

Before the round ended, I decided it was more than showmanship on Hagen's part. Putting his ball in trouble kept him from getting bored. One reason Hagen loved the seaside courses of Europe was that the winds and the uneven fairways made the game more interesting for a genius who grew tired of the ordinary good lies in most American fairways. In our exhibition, I would see a sparkle come to Hagen's eye when he faced an especially challenging shot.

When I hear golfers complain about bad lies, saying the breaks are going against them, I remember Hagen, who was excited by the challenge of his ball being behind a tree in the tall grass. Hagen looked upon a difficult recovery as an opportunity to thrill himself and the fans and shake the spirit of an opponent.

I heard that a little boy stepped up to Hagen as he approached a drive that had come to rest beside a bush. "I'm sorry you keep getting such bad breaks, sir," the boy said.

"Thank you, son," Hagen replied, smiling. "But regardless of the breaks, there my ball lies, and from there I will have to play it."

Forty More Yards for Bobby

MY SON, TINSLEY, was a member of the Future Farmers of America. One summer day in 1951 I was standing outside the clubhouse of our Riverside Drive course, watching one of Tinsley's cows eating the grass by the barn, when I became aware of a slim young man who was trying to catch my eye.

"Mr. Penick, my name is Bobby Moncrief. I want to play golf for you," he said.

"How much do you weigh?" I asked.

"One hundred and eighteen pounds," he said.

I said, "Wait here a minute."

Inside the golf shop I picked out a 7-iron and a 3-wood off the rack. I took the clubs back outside and handed them to Bobby.

"Swing those clubs for me," I said.

"You mean go to the range?"

"No, just swing the clubs. One at a time," I said.

As Bobby swung the clubs, he told me he had played last

year on the freshman team at SMU, but he wanted to go to school in Austin.

"I like this 3-wood," Bobby said, swinging it outside the golf shop. "I always hit a 3-wood off the tee in high school. Last year I finally started using a driver because I just absolutely had to have another twenty-five yards."

"How far do you hit your driver?" I asked.

"About 235 when my cleats come off the ground."

I asked if he was enchanted by distance or if he ever practiced his short game.

"Yes sir, my short game is good. I was such a short hitter off the tee in high school that I had to develop a good short game to win. My short game is accomplished."

"Never take your short game for granted," I said. "Keep practicing it above all."

He said, "Yes sir," and stood waiting.

I said, "I'd never take a boy away from SMU, but if you go to school in Austin I want you on my golf team."

I hadn't seen Bobby hit a ball, but I had seen his swing and looked into his eyes. I could see he was a player.

"There's only one thing I can give you, if you come here," I said.

"I'm not asking for anything," he said.

"I don't mean illegal inducements."

"What, then?"

I said, "I'll give you forty more yards off the tee."

Bobby made the top six the next spring in our qualifying tournament. He played with good players like Lee Pinkston, Wesley Ellis, Joe Bob Golden, and Fred Blackmar. Fred was the national left-hander champion and the father of Phil Blackmar, who plays on the tour.

I got busy with Bobby on the practice range. We concentrated on timing. Timing is different from rhythm and tempo. My dictionary says timing is the regulation of speed to produce the most effective result. I don't know how else to explain timing other than to say timing is hitting the ball at the right time in your swing. A swing could be rhythmic and have beautiful tempo but hit the ball at the wrong time. You see a lot of players with beautiful swings who are short hitters. They usually have poor timing. I think you are born with good timing. You see a bunch of kids in a boxing gym hitting the light bags, and you can tell which ones were born with timing and which are trying to develop it.

Bobby Moncrief was born with it.

I made him a short lecture before we began to discuss his forthcoming increase in distance. I said, "Stay under the ball and behind it. If you get out in front of the ball, you lose your power. You will find if you stay under, you will stay behind."

He knew what I meant by under. I meant swing under instead of over.

In a short time, Bob was hitting 270-yard drives. All he needed was the picture—under and behind.

When he comes to visit, he always reminds me of under and behind. That image is still his swing thought after a long run as a top amateur.

He had it made into a sign: UNDER AND BEHIND.

One year Bobby broke his favorite driver, a persimmon Wilson, in a tournament out of town. He had it rebuilt, but the new driver felt different from the one he loved.

When he returned to our club on Riverside, I walked out on the range to watch him hit his new driver.

Bobby hit four of the wildest rainbow slices I ever saw at any driving range.

"Let me have that driver," I said.

I took out my penknife, cut off the plastic band at the top of the handle, and then used the knife to peel off the grip. Underneath the leather grip was a piece of cork that covered the shaft.

"It's fixed," I said.

Bobby placed his hands on the cork, waggled a couple of times, and hit a long drive as straight as you could draw it with a ruler.

I said, "Your grip was too big. Your hands are fast, and the big grip was making you leave the club behind."

Over the years Bobby has told dozens, maybe hundreds, of people that I have wizardry powers. He used the driver story as his example.

But it's not wizardry. It's my craft. When you have seen many thousands of hands gripping golf clubs for decades, and you know the swing of the player you're observing, it is a simple thing to see a grip that does not fit.

Be Mindful

GOOD PLAYERS HAVE the power to think while they are competing. Most golfers are not thinking, even when they believe they are. They are only worrying.

Worrying is a misuse of your mind on the golf course. Whatever your obstacle, worry will only make it more difficult. Further, it is impossible to make a good golf swing if your muscles are too tense.

Rather than worrying, be mindful of the shot at hand and go ahead and play it as if you are going to hit the best shot of your life. You really might do it.

Three Most Common Faults

THE THREE MOST common faults I see among high handi-cappers are:

1. They aim to the right of their target.
2. They come over the top, which is a natural result of aiming to the right.
3. They keep their heads down too long.

Practice It First

DURING A LABOR DAY tournament at Austin Country Club, one of my college boys, Davis Love, Jr., hit his approach shot into a bunker on the first hole.

The ball was buried. Davis looked at it from all angles, but there was no way around it. He had to hit the ball out of the sand. It's the rules.

Davis blew it over the green and made a bogey.

On the second tee, I walked over to Davis and asked, "Do you practice that buried-lie shot very much?"

"No, Coach, I never practice it," he said.

"Davis, for the rest of this tournament I want you to stop hitting your approach shots into bunkers," I said. "You're li-

The University of Texas has had only three golf coaches:
Harvey, George Hannon, and Jimmy Clayton.

able to get another buried lie, and I don't want you to hit that shot again until you have practiced it."

Later that afternoon, I saw Davis in a practice bunker hitting ball after ball from buried lies. He became an expert at that shot. But not without practicing it now and then.

Treat the Easy Ones with Respect

I WAS SITTING in my cart under the oak trees at our course beside the river, watching a woman touring pro who was practicing on our putting green. She didn't know I was watching. I was supposed to give her a putting lesson, but sometimes I like to hide and observe for a while first.

As I was peeking from behind the trees, she missed ten consecutive three-foot putts. Every putt was missed one or two inches to the right of the hole. I had never seen anything like it.

"Are you doing that on purpose?" I called to her.

She looked around and saw me driving toward her out of the trees.

"Did you see me miss those putts?" she said.

"I could hardly believe my eyes."

"I just couldn't get lined up," she said.

I stopped my cart in the thick grass beside the green.

I said I hadn't ever noticed that she stepped back and looked at the line from behind the ball before any of her missed putts.

"It's only a three-footer," she said. "This isn't the Open."

"It still counts a stroke both here and at the Open," I

said. "Promise me you will always step back and approach every putt from behind for the rest of your life, whether it's practice or the real thing."

"Okay," she said.

"Now, let's repeat this procedure with ten consecutive three-foot putts."

I squared up her stance and made sure her eyes were straight above the ball, and told her the backward and forward stroke should be the same length.

"But the main point is, never take a short putt for granted. Always approach the ball from behind, and make a practice stroke or two, and hit your putt on the sweet spot," I said.

Doing it this way she sank ten in a row.

"Watch me hit some longer putts," she said.

I said, "No, that's enough to think about for one lesson. Treat every putt with respect. Always stick with your entire putting plan for each putt. Always take care with each and every putt, no matter how easy it looks. Call this a lesson that will save you many strokes over a lifetime."

Bibb's Cure for Lungers

MY OLD FRIEND Bibb Falk took Shoeless Joe Jackson's place in left field for the Chicago White Sox in 1920, the year after the Black Sox Scandal at the World Series caused Jackson to be thrown out of the game for life.

After a long and successful pro baseball career, Bibb came to the University of Texas as baseball coach in 1940. Two years later he went away to war, but he returned to coach at Texas for another twenty-odd years, making twenty-five in all.

One reason I mention the number of years Bibb coached is that I was golf coach at Texas for thirty-three years, ending in 1963.

Bibb's teams and my teams each won twenty Southwest Conference championships. Bibb won two national championships, and as coach I had one national intercollegiate champion, Ed White.

Bibb loved golf. He was one of the wildest hitters off the tee I ever played with regularly. Bibb got a thrill out of hitting home runs, to left, center, or right.

I went to see his teams play at the old Clark Field, our wonderful little ballpark on the campus that had a hill running up the fence in center field.

One afternoon I dropped by to watch Bibb put his team through a practice. I always thought observing great coaches was a path toward becoming one.

There was a tall, skinny outfielder at the plate taking batting practice. The boy had a good eye and could make contact with the ball, but he lunged forward when he hit it and thus lost his power.

This is such a common problem in golf that I was curious how Bibb would deal with it in his own sport.

I have written about Leaping Lucifer, the worst lunger I ever saw. This boy at Texas was not in that category, but he was persistent in his lunging. Bibb decided he had seen enough.

Bibb sent one of his student assistants off to find a length of clothesline where they hung the uniforms to dry. He instructed the batter to tie one end of the rope around his waist.

Bibb wrapped the other end of the line around both of his powerful hands and stood about twenty feet behind the hitter.

"Throw him one down the middle!" Bibb yelled.

The pitcher threw the ball, the outfielder swung his bat and tried to lunge forward—but Bibb dug in his heels and yanked the boy backward, sort of like a rodeo cowboy roping a calf.

"Throw him another!" Bibb yelled.

Again the pitcher threw, and this time the batter hit the ball solidly over second base, lunging a little less than before.

"You getting the idea? You stay home and hit the ball," Bibb said.

"Yes sir, I'm getting the idea," the boy replied.

Bibb stayed there for half an hour holding on to the clothesline tied around the boy's waist, as a couple of different pitchers stepped up to throw batting practice.

The boy learned. By the time Bibb ordered him untied, the boy was keeping his weight centered over the plate when he hit the ball instead of chasing out in front and losing his distance.

The boy said, with a big grin, "Coach, it's so much sweeter when I don't lunge."

For all these years since that time, I have remembered how Bibb cured the lunger. I have seen thousands of golfers who would have been helped greatly, I believe, by Bibb's method with the baseball player.

No, I have never done it. I have held the butt of a club against a player's head to keep it steady during the swing. I have stuck a shaft in the ground next to the pupil's left leg to show that the lunge would knock it over.

But I have never tied clothesline around a lunger's waist and ridden the pupil like livestock to haul back the forward leap.

For one thing, I weighed about 135 pounds in my prime, and I've seen golf lungers who could jerk me off my feet and drag me through the grass.

But the main reason I never did it is that it just doesn't seem like a proper thing to do.

I suppose the golf magazines will someday carry advertisements featuring the new miracle invention, a rope you can slip around your waist and wrap the other end around a telephone pole and cure your lunge. It was Bibb's idea.

You're On Your Own

HARRIS GREENWOOD PLAYED on my golf team in college, played in the U.S. Amateur, and then quit the game for about twenty-five years.

When he got the urge to take golf up again, Harris came to see me at our new course by the river.

"It's been so long since I've had a club in my hands that I can't remember how I used to swing," he said.

"Who would you want to swing like?"

I thought Harris would say Sam Snead. When he was in college, Harris's swing came over the top just a tad, as Snead's does.

"I want to swing like Ben Hogan," Harris said.

I looked at him and shook my head.

"Harris," I said, "I can't help you. Ben had to figure out his swing on his own, and if you want to swing like Ben, you'll need to resolve it for yourself."

Certainly I do not denigrate the swing of one of the top golfers in history. Ben's swing in his prime was awesome to watch.

I played with Ben when he was a young man with a big hook. I watched him change from a hooker to a fade, from a tough little competitor to a legend of the game. Ben did figure out his championship swing on his own to fit his particular physique and personality and enhance his own virtues while blocking out his flaws.

I couldn't teach Ben's swing to anyone. Millions have tried to copy it. A few, like Gardner Dickinson and George Knudson, came very close.

I would never try to teach a pupil to copy the swing of a genius. I always tried to give my pupils knowledge of the swing through mental pictures and muscular sensations, and we would hope for the pupil's own individual genius to emerge.

Hit the Can

SUPPOSE YOU ARE strolling along the road with a walking stick in your hand. You see an old tin can in the road. You decide on impulse to give the can a hearty two-handed whack that will knock it into the grass.

How do you do it? Do you tense up and worry about keeping your head still? Of course you don't, but your fundamentals are always sound when you whack a tin can.

That's the freewheeling feeling you should have when you hit a golf ball.

Saving the Cow

AUSTIN HAS GROWN large now, and 45th Street is in the central part of town. In my early years as head pro, 45th Street was the north boundary of Austin. Our country club, the second oldest west of the Mississippi, was several hundred yards south of 45th Street. We were out in the country. It was beautiful out there, with pure, flowing creeks and giant oak trees, and fields of wildflowers in the spring.

A German family had a farm down the road from the club. A blue northern hit us early one September, which is ordinarily a good golfing month in Texas. The creeks became solid hunks of ice. Oak tree limbs cracked and broke under the weight of ice. We stoked up the stove in the golf shop and our regulars huddled around it.

A member came in and said the German family was having a problem with one of the cows at their farm. Because of the slippery ice, they couldn't get the cow into their barn. The German farmers had studied the situation. They had decided to wrap a thick blanket of hay around the cow and cover her with a tarp.

For the next week our members sat around the fire and waited for the weather to break and pondered what should be done about the cow. The owners were bringing food and water every day, but still the ground was too slippery for the cow's hooves to traverse the ice all the way to the barn.

Over the history of our club, most of the great men of Texas have passed through. We've had the most powerful politicians, the richest tycoons, the brainiest professors and

Supreme Court Justices among our membership or as guests.

While the ice storm lasted, I cleaned and polished club-heads and shaved a number of hickory shafts. I would step into the front of the shop and hear my members discussing that stranded cow as they watched the long icicles draping the trees.

Many plans were hatched to deal with that cow. Straps and trusses and teams of mules were suggested. Finally it was decided that the wisest course was to let the cow stay where she was until the ice melted.

After six or seven days, one of our members struggled through the ice into the golf shop with the news that the cow was safe in the German family's barn.

"How'd they do it?" the hot stove crowd wanted to know.

"I hear one of our caddies showed up and tied gunny-sacks over the cow's hooves and just walked her home."

Jimmy Would Have Changed His Grip

DURING OUR MANY years as friends and colleagues, Jimmy Demaret and I had countless conversations about the golf grip. You may be surprised to discover that when Jimmy was Masters champion and known the world over for his ability, he decided his grip was wrong—but he was too far into a successful career to think seriously about changing it.

Jimmy used the familiar Vardon, or overlapping, grip from his early days as a caddie all the way to the end of his life. Yet he came to believe the Vardon grip is not the most fundamentally sound grip for most players, including Jimmy himself.

Harry Vardon made the piggybacking of the pinkie finger of his right hand onto the top of his left index finger—or into the space between the index and third fingers—into the most popular way for players to hold the club.

Vardon had big, strong, fast hands, and his style of grip was meant to move his hands closer together and, by removing one finger from the handle, reduce the possibility of his right hand overpowering his left during his swing. Proper application of his hands increased his power and helped him to control the club.

"But how many golfers do we encounter whose big problem is having too much power?" Jimmy would say.

Jimmy believed the average player should learn the so-called ten-finger grip. In fact, it is eight fingers and two thumbs, but you know what I mean.

This is often called the baseball grip, which is incorrect. If you were to grip a golf club like a baseball bat, your thumbs would be around the handle just as your fingers are.

"The full-fingered grip is the most fundamentally sound grip for the vast majority of golfers," Jimmy said. "Most golfers don't need to fight hands that are too fast. Most golfers have just the opposite problem—their hands are not fast enough."

In the full-fingered grip, Jimmy believed, the hands should be as close together as possible, with that right pinkie finger on the handle of the club to help deliver the blow.

"In a reasonable swing, the right hand won't take over from the left with the full-fingered grip," Jimmy said. "The two hands will work together. You get more power and better control. I'm so accustomed to the Vardon grip by now that it would take me a long time to change, and I'm doing

Harvey's grip, 1938.

okay the way things are. But if I was a newcomer to the game, or an average player who doesn't depend on golf for a living, I would certainly use the full-fingered grip."

Some top players use the full-fingered grip. Johnny Revolta, Bob Rosburg, Art Wall, Beth Daniel, and Alice Ritzmall come to mind. Johnny said he felt the full-fingered grip helped him stay behind and inside the ball and also made his release through the shot free and full. Alice was at a disadvantage when she first went on the tour because of her lack of length off the tee. I asked her to try the full-fingered grip. She did and her distance picked up considerably.

Looking back on my teaching career, I believe now that I should have taught the full-fingered grip to nearly every woman pupil, with the exception of powerful hitters like Babe Zaharias and Mickey Wright.

Perhaps I should have taught it to more men, as well. The full-fingered grip, with the hands properly placed, can be just as pretty to my eye as the Vardon grip.

There is no doubt that putting that one extra finger on the handle will supply a bit more authority when your clubhead whips through the ball.

Like Jimmy, I grew up as a caddie using the Vardon grip because it was the most popular grip among the players I watched and copied. I love the Vardon grip. I have taught it with great care for a very long time.

But if you are having trouble putting a solid smack on the ball, give the full-fingered grip a try. Watch that you hold your club lightly, especially with the right. Put your right thumb on the left side of the handle, where it can't jump in and take over your swing.

Thinking about Jimmy, I recall that he took golf lessons from only one man in his entire life. That man was the revered teacher Jack Burke, Sr., at River Oaks in Houston. As a youngster, Jimmy went to work for Jack as an assistant in the golf shop. Jack told Jimmy one of the benefits of the job was that Jimmy could play golf at River Oaks all he wanted.

"Just so long as you do it before six in the morning," Jack said.

Look Again

———

ON THE FOURTEENTH green at the Masters one year, Jackie Burke, Jr., had a twenty-foot putt that needed to roll over a hump on its way to the hole.

Jackie studied the putt. His caddie studied the putt. Finally his caddie straightened up and said, "It breaks about a foot."

"Which way?" Jackie asked.

"Well, now I have to look again," said his caddie.

Strike a Match

———

ONE TEACHING AID I used to use was a box of kitchen matches.

I would escort one of my college players out to the asphalt parking lot, open the box, and scatter kitchen matches on the ground.

Then I would tell the college boy to take his 7-iron and strike fire from those match heads with his golf swing.

This was a sure cure for hitting behind the ball and also a great aid to concentrating on the point of your aim.

If your mind wandered, you could sprain your wrist or put a nasty mark on the bottom of your club.

I used the kitchen matches on Betty Jameson when she first came to me for lessons, and later I did it with Mickey Wright, also.

Betty and Mickey could make that asphalt parking lot look like the Fourth of July.

The two of them hit the ball exactly at the bottom of their swings more precisely than any golfers I have ever seen. They could really strike those matches.

Not Quite Gentlemen

DURING MY YOUTH as a caddie, golf professionals were not allowed to enter the clubhouse through the front door, or to be seen in the dining room. Golf professionals were regarded as curious persons but not as gentlemen fit to mingle with proper society.

Walter Hagen arrived on the scene with his powerful charm and his champion's game, and things began to change around him.

Inverness was the first club to invite professionals into the clubhouse. I heard about it as a sixteen-year-old caddie.

After the U.S. Open in 1920, Hagen and a few other professionals presented the Inverness Club with a tall, chiming clock, set into a handsome wood stand with a poem on a brass plate.

The poem says:

God measures men by what they are,
Not in what wealth possess.
This vibrant message chimes afar
The voice of Inverness.

Salute from a Friend

IT WAS A SHOCK to all of us when Jimmy Demaret passed away suddenly. Jimmy had friends all over the world. Not only was he a champion golfer, he was a singer, a comedian, a good companion, and a person with a big heart.

I have a copy of a letter written by Ben Hogan as a salute to Jimmy, who was probably the best friend Ben ever had among his fellow golfers. Tears come to my eyes every time I read the letter, especially the last two paragraphs, which I quote:

"As partners, you and I never lost a four ball match, and, although I will be a little tardy in joining you, I want you to keep practicing so that one day we can win another four ball together.

"I send to you my admiration and thanks for all the nice things you have done for me and others—you helped make my bad times more bearable and my good times better. You were my friend and I miss you. May you sleep in peace and I will join you later."

Willie the Weeper

IN MY CADDIE days there was a boy in the yard named Willie. He was about twelve years old, wore bib overalls, and lived in a cabin on Shoal Creek with his folks, who made a living chopping cedars and catching catfish.

Willie was a good caddie. He was known for never losing a ball. Off the first tee the carry was over a flower garden and a road in those days, and Willie always found his player's ball if it was topped or popped up. He was in steady demand and sometimes was tipped as much as fifteen cents, which before World War I was big money to a kid.

But Willie was never happy. As far as Willie was concerned, the weather was always too hot or too cold, too wet or too dry, too windy or too still. The bread that he brought from home had too much butter on it, or not enough.

He usually had a headache. His feet hurt. Nothing was just the way he wanted it to be. My big brother, Tom, was the boss among the caddies. Tom got fed up listening to Willie's complaints and probably would have run him off except that Willie was popular with members. Willie never opened his mouth around a member, but he seldom shut it in the caddie yard.

Some of the boys started calling him Willie the Weeper.

To hear Willie tell it, he never had any luck, either. The breaks always went against him. Providence had a grudge against Willie, in his point of view. Life was not fair.

One morning in the caddie yard under a mighty oak tree, Willie was swinging at small stones with an old hickory-shafted niblick a member had given him. One of the small

stones turned out to be the tip of a large rock that was buried in the earth. The hickory shaft snapped in half.

"Look at that, will you?" Willie wailed. "Why does everything bad have to happen to me? It isn't fair!"

My brother, Tom, had a commanding presence, even as a boy. He walked over to Willie and said, "You want to change your life?"

"I want to get lucky, if that's what you mean."

"There's two things you've got to understand," Tom said. "The first is, nobody ever promised you life would be fair. The second is, to change your life you have to change the way you think."

Willie looked at the expression on Tom's face and decided not to complain about anything at that moment. A few days later Willie's folks packed up and moved farther out into the Hill Country, and I never saw him again. I heard he joined the Marine Corps and served in France.

I don't know if Willie took Tom's words to heart.

However, I do know that I never forgot them.

Too Far Forward

IN MY OPINION, most golfers play the ball too far forward in their stance.

This is one of the main reasons for average golfers to swing from the outside to the inside—they are trying to catch up to the ball position. I've heard many professionals comment that their ball position keeps creeping forward, and they have to stop and make themselves play it farther back.

Solid

My son, Tinsley, brought me a book that breaks the golf swing down into fifty-some "simple steps."

I studied the book. I have no quarrel with anyone who loves to examine golf in a scientific way. If you need to break the swing down into fifty-some positions, this book does a good job of it.

My approach is different.

I try to teach a swing that is all one motion that cannot be broken down into positions or else it will cease being one motion. My ideal is to teach my pupil to hit the ball solidly with his or her own best personal swing.

Solid is what you want in golf.

Check Your Hips

Hundreds of seasoned players have come to me with suffering and confusion written on their faces and have voiced the plaintive complaint that usually begins, "I have forgotten how to play golf. After all these years, my swing has left me. I feel as if I have never picked up a golf club in my life."

These are usually middle handicappers, and often they are middle-aged, as well, but this malady can strike any golfer of any age, even the experts and the young.

The first thing I do is reassure them. "Your swing hasn't left you," I say. "Something has inserted itself between your golfing mind and your muscles, and we had best get busy and find out what it is."

In most cases I have already guessed what is the root of the problem, and how to cure it, but I always start at the beginning by taking a look at the pupil's grip and address. If the grip and address are all right, then I am pretty sure that the problem is caused by a golf tip that has been so overdone that it has caused the pupil to forget one of the basic aspects of the swing—the turning of the hips.

It happens all the time. A pupil will read in a book or a magazine, or perhaps see on a television instructional, that such and such a thing should be done—like, perhaps, taking the club straight back from the ball for the first few inches—and this tip will appear to work wonders instantly.

So the pupil will concentrate on this tip to the exclusion of nearly all else, and the first thing you know, the pupil's golf swing has become a total stranger.

As I always say, golf tips are like aspirin. One may do you good, but if you swallow the whole bottle you will be lucky to survive.

Some fashionable teachers today stress a big shoulder turn with the hip turn severely limited. This, they say, creates a windup, a powerful tension between the shoulders and the hips that, when unleashed, creates tremendous power.

This is true, but it also creates the lower back pain that afflicts so many golfers, expert and dub alike.

Take the word of Bobby Jones or Ben Hogan, whose swings look very different but who agree that the biggest difference in ball striking between the good player and the high handicapper is most often in the use of the hips.

Pupils frequently tell me, "But it says in all the books that the hips should turn forty-five degrees and the shoulders ninety degrees."

That is fine, but too many players make an effort to hold their hip turns to forty-five degrees and wind up with no hip turn at all.

If you feel that your swing has gone away to some mysterious place, that the smack of authority has vanished from your golf, I am going to say right now that it is probably because you are not turning your hips.

If you make a good, full hip turn, both backward and forward, your swing will come back and the authority will return along with it.

One way to make a good hip turn is to turn your belly button to the right until you can feel your weight on your right heel, and then turn your belly button to the left until it is pointing at your target and your weight is on your left foot.

Another way to start the hip turn is by turning your right hip pocket backward until it almost faces your target.

However you decide to do it, be sure you make a turning motion, a rotation of the hips, and not a rocking motion that transfers your weight from one foot to the other without actually turning at all. I see this much too often.

I like to tell my pupils to turn as if shaking hands with someone on each side. It's the "Howdy do?" move.

Just make sure your belly button goes along on the ride. In fact, your belly button should be the engine that drives the movement.

Always remember, if your golf swing is not performing but your grip and stance are all right, check your hips.

Who Is Talking Here?

When I first started doing lectures in front of my peers at PGA teaching seminars, I was very nervous. I began many of these sessions with the old story about the fellow whose neighbors decided he was so obnoxious that they would tar and feather him and ride him out of town on a rail. After they had smeared him with tar and layered him with feathers and boosted him onto the rail, he looked down at them and said, "To tell you the truth, if it weren't for the honor of this occasion, I would just as soon walk."

What I told my fellow pros was that if it weren't for the honor of being at the podium, I would just as soon—in fact, I would rather—be sitting in the audience, listening to someone else. I enjoyed listening to other teachers, because I already knew what I was going to say unless they taught me something that was new to me.

I felt awkward about using the pronoun "I." Jimmy Demaret followed me onto the stage once and told the crowd, "Do you realize we have been listening to this man for more than an hour, and he has never once said 'I'?"

This was a problem for me. I didn't like to say "I," but it's awfully hard to talk all day without doing it.

Today many celebrities, especially athletes, solve this "I" problem by referring to themselves in the third person, almost as if the athlete and the speaker were two different people. But this sounds rather silly to me, and, besides, if I had said, "Harvey Penick thinks you should do so-and-so," the other pros would have laughed me out of the room for being so pompous.

I wasn't the only teaching pro who worried about using "I" too much.

Eventually, some of the pros started saying "we," instead, when speaking of themselves as individuals. I decided this was a sign of modesty. I got to where I would actually say, "Please excuse us, we have to give a lesson." Or, "Next week, we will be away, as we are playing in a tournament in Fort Worth." It may have sounded like a prize fight manager telling his fighter, "Don't worry, they can't hurt us." But I went along, blissfully unaware of my misuse of this royal "we."

Then one day I read an article by Mark Twain. The famous humorist said, "There are only three kinds of people who have a right to say 'we' when they mean 'I.' The first is the head of a state or nation. The second is an editor. And the third is a person with a tapeworm."

After I read that, I went back to using "I."

Use a Tee

I BELIEVE YOU should always use a tee on a par-three hole, simply because the tee gives you an advantage. I know there are many wonderful players, like Roberto DeVicenzo, who just toss a ball onto the grass at a par-three tee—and sometimes at a par four—and go ahead and strike an excellent shot. But I still believe you should make use of the extra edge you get by using that little wooden peg.

One of my Texas team players refused to use a tee. This boy was a fine golfer who thought he didn't need a peg. He thought using a tee was a sign of inferiority, and he shrugged off my suggestions that he might be an even better player if he would use the tee as the rules allow.

Finally one day I remarked to him, "You know, Bobby Jones never used a tee when he was young."

"Is that right?" my boy said, as if at last I had justified him.

I said, "Yes. But when Jones became a great champion, he always used a tee."

My player changed his habit that very day.

One warning about using tees, though. You may want to tee the ball high on a par four when you will hit it with a driver on the upswing for maximum distance. But on a par three, tee the ball low. All you are using the tee for is to give yourself a perfect lie.

I see too many high handicappers who tee the ball half an inch high to hit it with a medium iron on a par three, and the result is usually a poor shot. A ball that is teed high might look easy to hit with an iron, but that is an illusion.

Brownie

————

AT OUR CLUB near Riverside Drive we had a dog named Brownie who hung out around the place and loved to ride around the course beside me in a golf cart. Most people at the club liked Brownie, but her admirers did not include our greens superintendent.

The reason for this was that Brownie was constantly at war with the ground squirrels who lived on the course. When Brownie spotted a ground squirrel, she would leap out of the cart, chase the squirrel into its tunnel, and then begin at once to dig a big hole. The dirt would go flying out from Brownie's paws faster than a man could move it with a shovel.

Our greens superintendent kept asking that something be done about Brownie.

Billy Penn came up with the solution.

At a meeting of the board of directors, Penn brought up the motion and the vote was carried—making Brownie an honorary member of Austin Country Club.

For the Tall Player

THERE ARE SOME top golfers who are very tall people— George Archer, Andy North, Tom Weiskopf, young Ernie Els, and others—but the average player who is much above six feet tall has always been considered to be at a disadvantage because at address he is so much farther from the ball.

The two things that I stress for tall pupils are balance and tempo.

Balance is important to any player, but especially so for the tall. There is a center of balance—some call it gravity— for the golf swing that is generally believed to be somewhere near the belly button. Shorter players are able to turn this center during their swing with much more ease than taller players, whose long legs and long arms often struggle trying to coordinate with their hips.

The tempo of a tall player's swing must be smooth and at a speed that allows good balance in the feet, knees, and hips. Too fast a swing or any sudden movement in the swing can throw off the tall player's balance. Usually the tall player has a long swing that carries the clubhead fast enough that an effort to hit hard through the ball is not necessary.

The tall player must pay particular attention, too, to maintaining the same posture through the swing that was established at address. I see many tall pupils who can't resist the urge to dive toward the ball during the downswing and then suddenly bob upward, as if to correct this faulty movement.

Having clubs of the proper length can often correct this up-and-down move in the swing. But a tall player does not necessarily need longer clubs. The important measurement is from the hands to the ground, not from the top of the head to the ball. Sometimes short players with short arms need longer clubs than players who are a foot taller.

David Robinson, a pro basketball star who is more than seven feet tall, came to Golfsmith in Austin to have a set of clubs fitted to his requirements. Robinson snapped several shafts with his powerful swing during testing before the proper clubs were assembled for him—five inches above standard length.

The most important thing of all for a tall player is to learn to hit the ball solidly, which requires good balance and tempo. A long swing with good tempo and with solid contact will produce plenty of distance.

Tall players can look very graceful at golf. One of the most beautiful swings of all time is that of Tom Weiskopf, who is several inches over six feet. George Bayer, who is six feet five, in his younger days hit the ball as far as any man alive, and looked good doing it. I keep hearing a story—I even read it in a magazine—that I have been giving lessons to Michael Jordan, the basketball star, who is six feet six. I have never met Michael Jordan. Someone did phone the golf shop claiming to be him, but I doubt that it was. From this supposed call, the story began that Jordan had asked

Sign at the Austin Country Club, 1994.

what I would charge for a lesson, and I replied, "Five dollars and you furnish your own shag balls."

If he ever does call, I'll just tell him to come on and see me, no fee attached. I've watched Jordan play golf on television, and I'd like to watch him on the practice range.

Thoughts on Taking Dead Aim

ONE NIGHT AT a dinner party I heard a university professor remark that a chicken is an egg's way of making another egg.

I'd never thought about it that way before, but I realized at once that he was right. The egg came first, of course. We all come from eggs. Nobody arrives on earth full grown.

While they went on conversing at the table, my thoughts drifted to golf, and I knew that what the professor had said could be applied to teaching.

Inside every golfer there is an egg that we may say is where your golf swing comes from.

If it is an egg with a powerful, positive picture that calls forth right behavior, it will produce good play.

If it is an egg with negative thoughts and flawed motions that call forth wrong behavior, it can be changed by an act of faith.

Taking Dead Aim is an act of faith.

Steve Reid, who used to play on the PGA Tour, told me he was playing at Prestwick in Scotland one summer. Steve had hit a long drive onto the left side of the fairway, but the green was hidden by mounds of tall grass and bushes.

His caddie told him, "See that white house in the distance? Well, best you aim at the lower bedroom window on the right."

Steve whacked a long iron boring through the wind, apparently the shot of a lifetime. Grinning, Steve turned to the caddie expecting to hear, "Well done."

The caddie said, "Boonker."

"Boonker?" Steve yelled. "What do you mean boonker? I hit a perfect shot, right where you told me."

The caddie said, "Nae, I said the lower bedroom window on the right. You were one window too far left. You're in the boonker."

Steve told me that he thought he took aim until he started thinking about Taking Dead Aim—as evinced by the lower bedroom window on the right—and, "I realized by comparison to what that caddie wanted, I had played on the tour for years thinking I was aiming when really I was just aiming at the whole wide world."

When I ask you to Take Dead Aim, I mean that for a few seconds you should become calm but aware, putting all your best attention to the moment at hand. You make what I think of as the sweet calculations of wind and weather and distance, and see a sharp picture of your ball striking your target in your mind. Bobby Fischer, the chess champion, said that when it was his turn to play, he considered only one move—the right one. You take out the club your mind tells your muscles is the right one to swing. At this point your imagination is stronger than your willpower. Your body will do what your mind tells it to do. You have no doubt, no fear. For those few seconds you are what you think.

That's Taking Dead Aim. Trust yourself.

The "I" in Maxfli

EVER SINCE HE was new to teaching a number of years ago, Mark Steinbauer has showed up regularly to visit with me on the practice range at Austin Country Club or at home or during my spells in the hospital. I have always enjoyed talking with Mark. It has been a pleasure to watch him progress to where he is now director of golf for the big resort called The Woodlands in the pines near Houston.

On his most recent visit, Mark was discussing one type of person who can be a test of the teacher's patience. This is the person who always wants to know "why?" Mark calls them "analytical." I call them doctors, lawyers, accountants, and engineers, for the most part.

I remembered a judge who showed up one day for a lesson at the old club on Riverside Drive. It was in the shag ball days, and the judge brought a fat sack of balls with him. Everything I said to the judge, he would peer at me and frown and ask, "Why should I do that? Where does that fit in my total swing?"

Finally I said, "Judge, I'm going to tell you the real secret of golf."

I picked up one of his shag balls and showed it to him.

"See where it says Maxfli?" I said. "I want you to keep your eye on the 'i' in Maxfli. Think about that and that alone. The reason, as you can see, makes good sense. Walter Hagen always said that even as great a player as he needed to look at the ball when he hit it."

The judge began to hit the ball solidly almost at once and went away believing he knew the secret of golf. As long as this teaching got results for the judge, it truly was the secret of golf.

As I told Mark, keeping your eye on the ball is a teaching that will do no harm and may even be of great benefit, as it was to the judge. By keeping his eye on the "i" in Maxfli, he had something definite to concentrate on and could more easily exclude the many questions that rambled through his analytical mind.

A teacher must beware of what is said to a pupil. What the teacher says is the strongest thought in the pupil's mind and cannot be easily retracted.

The Masters Champion

IT WAS A JOYFUL drive to the airport with Helen in the spring of 1984. We were joining a group welcoming Ben Crenshaw back to Austin. In his bag he would be carrying the green jacket of a Masters champion. Ben had finished second in the Masters in 1983, but yesterday he had won it, one of the grandest prizes in golf.

Ben had been off his game for a while. He had a health problem, and there was a lot on his mind. I watched him play golf on television, and I wanted to visit with him. I started praying every night that Ben would come see me.

So of course he did come see me shortly before the Masters. We looked at his swing and checked his ball position, address, and clubface angle to see that they remained as they had always been. We talked about achieving a calm mind. I believe if you have the desire to win and you let

God's hand rest on your shoulder, if it is your turn to win, you will win.

"Just swing like Ben," I told him. I felt good about Ben when he left for the tournament. Ben led the first day at the Masters, and Tommy Kite took the lead by the end of the third round. Ben got the lead again on the tenth hole of the final day by sinking a sixty-foot birdie putt, his third birdie in a row. I was sad for Tommy, but I cried tears of happiness in front of my TV when Ben became the Masters champion, just as I did eight years later when Tommy won the U.S. Open at Pebble Beach. Tommy and Ben are like sons to me.

At the 1984 Masters, Ben showed he had faith in his own natural way. He trusted himself. That's what I was thinking about as Helen and I drove to the airport, and I couldn't wait to see Ben wearing that new green jacket.

Helen

THE MOST FORTUNATE day of my life was the Sunday morning I decided to go with my mother to the Hyde Park Christian Church, where she was a charter member. We sat in the back row that morning, but my eyes were drawn to a beautiful girl who was singing in the choir. I kept staring at her, hoping she would look back at me. After the service, I asked about her and found out her name was Helen Holmes. She was the daughter of a preacher who had moved from town to town, building a church wherever he went.

Helen had a teacher's certificate from Southwest Texas

State in San Marcos. She had moved to Austin to attend the University of Texas and to teach school. I found out where she lived and made plans to become acquainted with her. One day I dressed in my finest coat and tie and cap, wearing my new knickers, and borrowed my brother Tom's car. I pulled up near Helen as she was walking along the sidewalk and asked if I might give her a ride to school.

She said, "No."

A few days later I contrived to be where Helen was crossing the street. I introduced myself again and asked if she might allow me to phone her sometime. She said that would be okay. I waited fifteen minutes and called her and asked her to go with me to the Texas Open in San Antonio for a day.

Helen didn't know what a golf pro was, but she had never been to San Antonio and agreed to accompany me. When I went by to pick her up, she was the most gorgeous girl I have ever seen. The only thing wrong was she was wearing high heels. I worked up the courage to explain to her that she would have to change shoes, and we set off on the drive to San Antonio.

When we arrived at Brackenridge Park, Bob Hope and Bing Crosby were getting ready to tee off. Helen was excited. Seeing Hope and Crosby might have been what convinced her that golf must be a good game.

I knew Helen was the woman I wanted to spend my life with, but I was afraid her father might not let her marry a golf pro. Reverend Holmes was a good athlete and a fan of baseball and football. He told me golf looked like a simple thing. I took him to the club and gave him a lesson. He tried and tried, but he couldn't hit the ball. Finally he threw down the club and shouted, "Confound it!" That was the strongest language he ever used.

Within a year Helen and I got married. We lived in a

lovely home on Laurel Lane in Hyde Park, not far from the club. The President of the University lived down the street from us. Our daughter, Kathryn Lee, was born, and a few years later Helen became pregnant with our son, Tinsley. We needed another bedroom. The house directly behind us came up for sale, and we bought it. There was a huge oak tree in the front yard, locally famous as the "lying down oak" because it lay along the ground before it gently began to rise. Old timers told us Indians had bent that tree as a sapling and tied it down to point north. Tinsley's dog would hop onto the trunk and scamper up into the highest branches, the only dog I ever saw climb a tree.

Helen would always follow me when I played in a tournament. Critical remarks from the spectators would annoy her. One day after I had missed a short putt, I heard someone in the gallery say, "Why couldn't he make that one?" Then I heard Helen say, "If you think you can do any better, why don't you get out there and try it?"

In 1950 Austin Country Club moved from Hancock Park to a new location on the southeast edge of town near the Colorado River. Helen and I bought some land near the club, and she designed her dream home, which we built near the twelfth tee. Helen wanted to name our dirt road Tinlee Drive—after Kathryn Lee and Tinsley—but one morning the city came out and put up a sign naming it Penick Drive. We lived in that house for thirty-two years.

My brother, Tom, and I owned a driving range on land we bought where the Municipal Auditorium is now on the bank of the river. It was the only driving range in town and one of the few in Texas. Seven days a week, I would go to the club early in the morning and unlock the doors and stay until lock-up time in the evening. Then I would pick up Helen and we would go to the driving range. The long hours were

Helen and Harvey, 1994.

hard on both of us, and eventually Tom and I shut down the driving range.

My senior year in high school, while I was working in the golf shop, an influential member of the club had offered to get me an appointment to West Point. I told him, "No, thank you, sir. The only thing in life I want to be is a golf pro." I never regretted that decision, but later I did wonder if it was fair to Helen to be the wife of a club pro who was seldom at home. Helen, bless her soul, put up with me. I could not have lasted so long in this job without her love and support.

In 1972 I was driving too fast in a golf cart, heading for the barn where I heard vandals were wrecking the place, and I hit a bump and fell out and broke my back. Of all the ways for me to get hurt! I was always opposed to golf carts, and now one of them had almost killed me. Every day and night for the rest of my life, I have been in pain. Helen takes care of me.

As my brother, Tom, had taught me, life was not created for the sole purpose of making me comfortable. I learned it was better to meet the pain head on and go about my business than to try to hide from it behind pills and self-pity. But without Helen, I might have given up.

When our new Pete Dye course opened on the northwest side of town, Helen and I moved again. By now Tinsley was the head pro. I was called the head pro emeritus, which in fact meant I was the starter at the first tee. I used to laugh and say, "In only sixty years I have managed to work my way into the worst job at the club."

And all this time, through all the long hours and the sickness, Helen has stood by me and given me strength. She is the most wonderful, courageous person I have ever known. I thank God for sending me to the Hyde Park Christian Church that day so long ago, and I thank Helen for sharing her life with me.

Any time a young pro has asked me what is the most important thing to learn, I always say, "The most important thing, if you are lucky enough, is to marry the right person."

I did. I love you, Helen.

Epilogue

During the week of the 1995 Ryder Cup in Rochester, New York, there was an event held to honor Harvey Penick. Many of golf's top teachers were on the program. The keynote speaker was Tinsley Penick, Harvey's son, who more than twenty-five years earlier had replaced his father as head pro at Austin Country Club.
This is That Tinsley said.

GOOD EVENING. I'd like to thank Dan Parks for honoring my father here tonight and for staging this wonderful event. I'm flattered to be on the same program with these great teachers. These are some of the greatest names in golf in the latter part of the twentieth century. For me to appear with them is a great tribute to my father.

A friend of mine named Dick Harmon is the pro at River Oaks Country Club in Houston. One of his brothers, Craig, is the pro here at Oak Hill. They are sons of Claude Harmon, and they learned golf and teaching golf from their father. Dick says he thinks his father could start a sentence, and Dick could finish it.

I could say that about my father and myself. If my dad was right when he said he saw more golf shots than any man alive, then I've probably heard about more golf shots than any man alive.

Anyone who has been able to compare my father's teaching methods to those of the rest of the gentlemen on this program will probably notice a difference in approach.

My father's techniques might seem at odds with today's methods.

They're not high tech at all. They're very simple, sometimes frustratingly so.

Many people who took lessons from him wondered afterward what had happened.

Claude Harmon used to say about him, "It takes a lot of courage to teach like Harvey, to say as little as he does."

In fact, that was a deliberate part of my father's technique.

He reinforced a positive mental game, but did it in very subtle ways.

I think one of the reasons he is considered a great instructor is that he gave pupils confidence.

Dr. Tom Kirksey, an Austin cardiologist, took a lesson and later tried to figure out what Harvey had told him. Dr. Kirksey shook his head, couldn't figure it out. But whatever it was, it worked. Dr. Kirksey later said that a lesson from my father was sort of like reading the Old Testament—there's an important message there, but you're not sure what it is.

Many teaching pros will prefer giving a lesson to a high handicapper over a scratch player. It's much easier to help a beginner, and any advice you give a very good player runs the risk of having a negative effect. My father was very conscious of that. But he had his own way of teaching the good players.

For example, Hal Underwood, who had a tremendous career as an amateur and was on the tour for a few years in the early '70s, once took a lesson from my father. Hal hit a lot of balls for about half an hour on the practice tee with my dad watching him closely but not saying a word. Finally, when there were no more balls to hit, Hal asked my father, "Well, what do you think?" My dad stood there another minute or so and finally said, "I don't know. Let me think about it overnight." And he turned around and walked off.

The next day, my dad saw Hal at the club and said, "I've thought about it all night, and I don't recommend any change." Years later Hal is still amazed by the experience.

Few pros would dream of teaching like this. And most players today probably would demand more information. My father was famous for not changing anything about the golfer's swing, but not telling the golfer why.

My father inherited this technique from the methods of the old Scottish professionals who pretty much were the only instructors around in the early part of this century. Maybe the most famous of them was Stewart Maiden, who was Bobby Jones's instructor. There's a famous story about how Bobby was getting ready to play a tournament at Winged Foot and called Stewart in Augusta and asked him to come up and look at his swing. Stewart took the train to New York and met up with Bobby on the practice tee. He watched Bobby take a couple of swings and said, "You don't hit the ball with your backswing, laddie." Then Stewart walked off.

One of the better instructors in the Austin area, Chuck Cook, decided to take on a personal challenge once and try to teach like my father for one week. His first lesson was with Omar Uresti, who at the time was playing for the University of Texas team and is now on the tour. Chuck made a suggestion about Omar's grip, and didn't say anything about what the objective was. Omar asked him, "Why would you want me to do that?" Chuck tried to do what my father would have done and said, "Don't think about it, just do it." But Omar kept asking, and after a short while Chuck threw up his hands and went back to his usual way of teaching.

I'd like to think my father's techniques are timeless. For the most part, he was self-taught as an instructor. It's important to remember that my father was already caddying at Austin Country Club when Francis Ouimet won the U.S. Open in 1913. My dad talked about the time William

Howard Taft played the course and the Secret Service escorted the President around on horseback with their rifles. After my father became the pro in 1923, he was about the only recognized teaching pro in Texas for many years who was born in the United States.

My father did have some role models and some pros whose methods he greatly respected in his earlier years—especially Jack Burke, Sr., Bobby Jones, J. Victor East, who was also a club designer at Spalding, and Stewart Maiden.

In my opinion my father's greatest attribute was one that all great teachers have—complete confidence in himself. In his own mind he was absolutely sure he knew what was wrong with a golfer's swing. And that probably explains why his advice was so minimal much of the time—he wouldn't change a swing unless he was dead sure what the problem was.

The *Little Red Book* has a story about a lesson my father gave Don January to see if he was ready to join the tour. My father told him, "Don, some people are going to tell you that you're losing control at the top. Don't listen to them. Pack your bags and go to California and join the tour."

Sometimes his only advice would be something that would help the good player's frame of mind. He told Tom Kite when he joined the tour to go to dinner with good putters, the idea being that their confidence would be contagious. If you surround yourself with good, positive people, it will rub off on your game—and he applied that to other facets of life as well.

When Lanny Wadkins was at Austin Country Club earlier this year, my father told him that at one time he believed the turn in the golf swing was simply a way for the big muscles to get out of the way so the golfer could use the small muscles. Later on, after he had watched a lot of the modern pros on television, my dad decided it is best to use both the big and small muscles, as long as it is in the proper manner.

In fact, my father realized that many very successful players and instructors today have learned how to incorporate the whole body into the golf swing, and he accepted that. A swing like John Daly's would break many instructors' fundamentals. But my dad watched John on TV many times and would say, "I admire him because he found a swing that suits him. I'd advise him not to change it."

Seventy years as an instructor gave my dad a lot of experience to draw on. One day a vendor came to the club peddling a high-tech video machine. The salesman photographed my swing and printed it out in a series of sequence shots. I showed the prints to my dad.

He said, "That is really a high follow-through. How well did you hit it?"

I said, "I hit it good."

My dad said, "Horton Smith used to finish that high."

I think he was telling me a high finish is good if it works for me, but he had to go back fifty years to recall another finish as high as mine.

My father never bad-mouthed another instructor's methods. If a player was putting crosshanded, he might disagree but he would never say, "That's the stupidest putting stroke I ever saw." Instead, he would say, "It works for Bernhard Langer, but it might not work for you."

My father generally favored a strong grip. When Jack Nicklaus popularized the neutral grip, my father would say, "It works for Jack Nicklaus, but it might not work for most of us."

One of the fundamentals he taught was to position your eyes over the ball at address when putting. But when we were filming *The Little Green Video*, he decided he couldn't use that tip. Ben Crenshaw was doing the demonstration, and when Ben sets up, his eyes are not over the ball.

By the way, the filming of *The Little Green Video* was the first time that my father ever allowed Tom Kite to watch him give a lesson to Ben Crenshaw, or vice-versa. He understood how different the two players are, and he was concerned that a tip intended for one could subconsciously have a bad effect on the other.

A footnote about lifting the left heel on the backswing. My dad's preference was for the left heel to come off the ground. He gave Kathy Whitworth many, many lessons over the years. When Kathy was young, she used to drive to Austin from her home in New Mexico—at least a ten-hour drive—three or four times a month. She went on to make the LPGA Hall of Fame, and during her entire career she has never once lifted her left heel off the ground during the backswing, and my father never once said a word about it to her.

Before I close, here are just a few more examples of my father's teaching techniques. My father did not like for a pupil to warm up before a lesson. If they were hitting good, it could only get worse. If they were hitting bad, they would already have negative thoughts. My dad wanted to start fresh. My dad told his pupils to avoid weightlifting unless they were being instructed by someone who was qualified and who understood the golf swing. He also told people it wasn't a good idea to go swimming before playing golf.

On alignment, my father was more concerned with the player hitting the ball solid. He would say, "Don't worry about alignment until you start hitting solid. Then I'll tell you where to line up." He would remind pupils that Lee Trevino and Sam Snead line up thirty yards apart, Lee to play his fade and Sam to play his draw.

My father coached the University of Texas golf team for thirty-three years. He not only taught a lot of good young golfers, he also learned from them. He would always ask a new player about the methods and teaching techniques of his local pro. My dad gained a lot of knowledge from these experiences.

*The statue of Harvey and Tom Kite at the
Austin Country Club, dedicated April 2, 1995.*

My dad always said that the day he stopped learning would be the day he stopped teaching. He must have been learning right up to the day he died, because he never stopped teaching. You may have heard the story about Ben Crenshaw visiting my father in his bedroom a few days before he was to leave for Augusta this year. Ben told my father he was having a little trouble with putting.

My dad asked Ben, "Have you been taking a couple of practice strokes before each putt and imagining the ball going into the hole?"

Ben said, "You know, I don't think I have been."

My father said, "Get a putter and let me watch you take a few strokes on the carpet."

The lesson went on for about an hour.

Two weeks later, Ben won the Masters.

So if the question is, "Would Harvey Penick's methods work today?" I guess the answer is "Yes, they do."

Thank you all very much for the honor of being able to share a few memories with you.

Picture Credits

All photos courtesy of Tinsley Penick, with the exception of the following:

Page 23: *Sports Illustrated* Picture Collection
(Photo by Susan Allen Camp)
pages 92, 225: Austin Country Club Archives
page 204: AP/Wide World Photos
pages 218, 250, 326, 334, 343: Carrell Grigsby Photography
page 257: Painting by Paul Milosevich
page 268: Drawing by Betty Hicks
page 291: University of Texas